A Novel INTRODUCTION
TO
CORPORATE FINANCE

REVISED EDITION

BY JONATHAN GODBEY AND JASON MEHL

San Diego, CA

Bassim Hamadeh, CEO and Publisher
Christopher Foster, General Vice President
Michael Simpson, Vice President of Acquisitions
Jessica Knott, Managing Editor
Kevin Fahey, Cognella Marketing Manager
Jess Busch, Senior Graphic Designer
Zina Craft, Acquisitions Editor
Jamie Giganti, Project Editor
Brian Fahey, Licensing Associate

First published in the United States of America in 2013 by Cognella, Inc.

Trademark Notice: Product or corporate names may be trademarks or registered trademarks, and are used only for identification and explanation without intent to infringe.

Printed in the United States of America

ISBN: 978-1-62131-396-0 (pbk)

www.cognella.com 800.200.3908

CONTEN

CHAPTER 1

THE STORY OF CASPIAN SEA DRINKS

I

W hat if I got an intern?"
    "What? For what?"
"I don't know," said Sean Stovall. "I was just thinking."

"You spend," said William Toth, then swung a driver at a teed-up golf ball and watched the ball sail over the 50-yard sign, "I'll think."

William Toth was Sean Stovall's accountant. Stovall was a mid-level investor who'd been investing his portion of a large inheritance for ten years. He lived well—two houses with pools, expensive cars, boats—but he still felt poor. He was only maintaining a financial status established by his grandfather and his father. He'd employed accountants before and been unhappy with each one. He met Toth one day at breakfast with a friend and business associate. By noon the same day, he'd fired his current accountant, made Toth an offer, doubled it, and hired Toth away from his friend. Toth was young, energetic, and attached to nothing but his smart phone and his bottom line. Everyone who knew him knew that his loyalty was to himself alone, but looking out for himself required him to look out for the interests of his clients—wealthy investors who wanted more wealth.

"I talked to Eric Bensen last week. He said he's thinking of starting an internship program."

"Bensen? Where'd you see him?"

"It was a college alumni thing. You know him?"

"Caspian Sea? I know money. You know how much that guy's worth?"

"I don't wanna know."

"About thirty times more than you."

"You know what I'm worth?"

"I'm your accountant—he's worth 28.4 times more than you."

"You said 30."

Stovall and Toth were hitting golf balls at the driving range, each chewing on unlit cigars. Toth never touched cigars unless he was with Stovall, but he handled the cigar with more aptitude than Stovall who slobbered and spat repeatedly. Stovall had referred to himself more than once as a *cigar officia-dundo*.

"How do you even talk to that guy without puking?"

"What?"

"You told me the story two weeks ago. You bailed him out and got nothing in return."

"I gave my wife a Wimbledon honeymoon. I told you, it was the only way I could get the cash."

"There are so many things wrong with that." Toth swung and hit a ball then leaned on the driver he'd borrowed from Stovall. He didn't own a set of clubs, but hit golf balls harder and straighter than most of the clients with whom he played.

"Like what?"

"Like Wimbledon happens every year. Like Claudia wouldn't know a half-volley from a drop-shot, no offense. Like you bailed out a fledgling company—possibly, *probably* a dying company—and all you got was what? Eight thousand dollars? That's like five thousand pounds. Knowing you and Claudia, that barely paid for your Wimbledon lunches."

"I told you it was a mistake. What do you want?"

"I'm just saying, I know your bottom line. If I were you, I wouldn't sleep knowing that guy is rolling in it."

Toth lined up and took a swing and looked away from the ball before it landed. "You're doing fine and I'm gonna make sure you do better. But—" he bent down and teed up another ball, "I'm not saying you need to do anything, okay? *But*, if I were you, I'd wanna settle that somehow."

"What's to settle?"

"The fact that there's a company worth ten billion dollars that wouldn't exist without your blind, if not ignorant, generosity! Based on what you said, you've got no legal ground to expect anything from him—even if you did, it'd be tough to convince a judge at this point, especially going against the lawyers he'd be able to pay. And there's no way a businessman of his caliber is going to just throw you a chunk of gratitude money."

"Maybe I could get him to tell the story in some interview or something—give me some credit."

"Credit? That's not credit. Listen. There's no way you come off in that story as anything other than a loser. To Bensen you're a hero—that's why he still talks to you like you're his pal. But to anyone else, you're the guy who missed out on a big thing—you're the Trail Blazers picking Sam Bowie over Michael Jordan."

"So what are you saying?" Stovall asked. He leaned on his driver and stood still and watched Toth carry his driver over to the bag and switch it out for an iron. Toth didn't speak. He hit five balls and watched them all land and roll within several yards of each other. "You expect me to believe you don't own clubs?" Stovall asked.

"I'm thinking," Toth said without looking up. Stovall watched Toth knock over a new bucket of balls and begin hitting them toward various pins on the driving range. He figured Toth would talk when he was ready. He went back to chopping at his own bucket of balls.

Several minutes later Toth asked, "What is Caspian Sea anyway?"

"It's juice, kind of."

"Yeah, but it's confusing. It's purple and it's not grape? What's a sea anyway? An ocean? Why not call it an ocean?"

"It's selling."

"Yeah, but imagine how much more it would sell if it made sense—colors that matched flavors with a down home domestic name."

"He's already said he's not doing that. He's a purist or whatever."

"Fine. You don't *want* him to do it. *You* do it."

"How?"

"Using his formula, just tweak it."

"And how do I get his formula?"

"His new intern gives it to you."

"Who's his new intern? Why would he give her the formula? Why would she give it to me?"

"I'll figure all that out. I was thinking about a guy intern by the way—a girl might look like more fun, but it'd get too complicated."

"What? You're going to give him a fake intern and hope she can get the secret out of him and give it to us? Is that legal?"

"*He.* Is it legal? *Is it illegal? Mr. Bensen, did you give the formula to Johnny Intern?* What court in the land is going to convict a guy of car theft if the owner takes the stand and says, *I gave him my keys?*"

II

Eric Bensen, founder and CEO of Caspian Sea Drinks, was recently named Philanthropist of the Year by *The Caritas Response*. The honor was bestowed upon Mr. Bensen due primarily to his involvement with the Liquidity Foundation, which is dedicated to the strengthening of communities in the developing world. The original purpose of the foundation was to finance sustainable clean-water projects for individual communities in Africa. As more needs were identified in these communities, the foundation became involved in meeting those that were most prominent. With the help of Mr. Bensen's contribution, the Liquidity Foundation plans to continue its work with clean-water projects, while also helping to strengthen existing educational and medical facilities, provide educational opportunities for community leaders, and provide micro-finance opportunities for local entrepreneurs.

Mr. Bensen announced his most significant financial contribution to the foundation so far, $2 million, at a black-tie fundraiser for one of Liquidity's ongoing medical projects in East Africa. Derek Foster, a junior Finance major, volunteered to work as a waiter at the event. He was assigned to the top table. After maneuvering around tables and waiters and philanthropists and moguls for three hours, making countless trips between the kitchen and the high-profile table, Derek was wondering if he had wasted his Friday night.

When he learned he'd be serving Mr. Bensen, he anxiously thought of potential comments he could make which would lead to a conversation. But the evening was drawing to an end, he was tired, and Mr. Bensen had yet to show any interest in talking to him. No longer thinking about generating conversation, Derek brought dessert to the guests at his table. He carefully placed a slice of red velvet cake in front of Mr. Bensen who, for the first time all evening, spoke to him. "Thanks."

"My pleasure," said Derek.

"You work at Chick-fil-A?" Mr. Bensen asked.

"Excuse me?" Derek had thought about answers to a few potential questions, but that wasn't one of them.

"Do you work at Chick-fil-A?"

"No sir. Sorry, do you smell something?" Derek stood up straight.

"Smell?" Mr. Bensen turned to his left in his chair and looked confused at Derek.

"Do I have chicken hands?"

"Chicken hands?"

"Sorry, I just had a sandwich."

"They have Chick-fil-A back there?"

"No. Earlier. Before I got here."

"Don't they feed you guys here?"

"Probably, I don't know. I'm sure—maybe they do. They will. I think, maybe, later on ... I didn't wanna assume. I washed my hands though ... " Derek's right hand wobbled slightly, still gripping another plate.

"Relax, you don't smell like chicken. It was the *my pleasure* response. They're fond of that at Chick-fil-A. I wanted to ask you if they require employees to use it."

"Oh. Right. Yeah—yes sir. I don't know."

"Why don't you find that out and get back to me?" Mr. Bensen turned around to his cake.

"Right, yes sir. I will." Derek took a step behind Mr. Bensen and paused. "Is there, uh, how ... ?"

"I'm kidding."

"Ha. Yes sir, of course. Sorry." Derek served cake to the rest of the table and then went into the kitchen. "Chicken hands," he said to no one, and cursed himself for working the dinner.

Talking to Mr. Bensen, he felt foolish and inadequate. He hated when he did things for the wrong reasons, and he hated that he seemed unable to recognize the wrong reasons until after he'd committed to doing the things. He had to offer refills of coffee. He didn't want to try to talk to Mr. Bensen again. He wasn't sure if he should act as if he'd never talked to him, or if he should try to make a joke out of how he'd sounded like an idiot. He rehearsed possibilities in his head before returning to the table for coffee refills.

Mr. Bensen turned to his left again as Derek poured coffee into the cup of the man next to him. "Tell me your name," he said to Derek.

"Derek." Derek thanked God he hadn't said, 'Ole Chicken Hands.'

"Eric Bensen," he said and stuck out his hand.

"It's a pleasure, sir. I mean ... "

"You're volunteering here right?"

"Yes sir."

"Why?"

"Well, honestly? I'm following the advice of a professor."

"Really? You're at the college?"

"Yes sir."

"What kind of professor is he?"

"He's okay. Young guy, sort of."

"Math? History? Biology?"

"Sorry. Finance—Intro to Finance—An Introduction to Corporate Finance."

"Okay. Networking, huh? Bless you Derek. You're a good student, aren't you?" Mr. Bensen went for his wallet.

"Well—" Derek didn't know what to say.

"Here's your contact." Mr. Bensen held out a card for Derek. "Maybe he'll drop a quiz grade for you or something—extra credit. Not that you need it though, right?" Derek didn't respond. "Call and make an appointment. Come and tell me about Corporate Finance. I could use some of that."

"Seriously? Yes sir. Thank you, sir. Thanks."

Sean Stovall, sitting with his tanned and yoga-toned wife three tables away from the head table, had been watching Bensen all night. When he saw Bensen give a business card to Derek he nodded to himself like he'd just caught on to an old magic trick. When the dinner ended, Stovall approached the head table and waited for an opportunity to shake Bensen's hand.

"There he is!" said Bensen as they shook hands. "How are ya?"

"Good, man. Nice event—big night for you!"

"Yeah, thanks. Hey, wasn't I talking to you about the whole internship thing?"

"Yeah."

"I think I might've found my guy."

"Yeah? Who'd've thought you'd find some waiter you could mentor?"

"What do you mean?"

Stovall swallowed hard, realizing he might've just betrayed his awareness of Toth's plan. "I mean, is that the guy? That waiter guy I saw you talking to?"

"Yeah. Uh ... yeah. The waiter, I don't remember his name. He's a student, volunteering."

"Yeah, okay, good. I don't know his name either," Stovall said.

"Of course not," Mr. Bensen said, and looked confused. "Well, good seeing you."

"Yeah. Good. You too. See you around."

III

Derek made the phone call around lunch the following Monday and was given an appointment for Wednesday afternoon. He wondered what he should wear. He didn't own a suit—he'd had to rent one to wait tables at the dinner. He decided not to try too hard—he was a student, he'd dress like a student—a serious student. The next afternoon, as he looked out through the glass of the elevator lifting him twenty-three floors over the sea of suits swarming around the ground floor of the building, he second-guessed his decision. The elevator stopped. He stepped off and walked over and through the opening between floor-to-ceiling glass windows etched with the Caspian Sea logo.

"I have an appointment with Mr. Bensen," he said to the woman at the reception desk.

She smiled and pointed him through another opening behind her where an older woman sat behind another desk. She stood up. "Derek?" She stepped out from her desk and Derek walked over to her and shook her hand.

"Yes ma'am," he said.

"I'm Mrs. Howe. We talked on the phone. Nice to meet you." She stepped over and opened the door behind her. "Mr. Bensen's expecting you."

"Thanks," Derek said and stepped into the large office. Mr. Bensen stood up, walked around his desk and extended his hand, "Derek, good to see ya." They shook hands. "Have a seat." Mr. Bensen gestured toward a round wooden table in the opposite corner of the room.

"Thank you, sir." Derek sat in a chair that provided him with a view of the entire office, as well as a good portion of the city outside the windowed walls. He then said the first thing he'd planned to say, "My pleasure? Chick-fil-A? They do tell everyone to respond that way to anyone who thanks them."

"Really? They require it?"

"Yeah, well, they highly recommend it."

"What do you think about that?"

Derek answered Mr. Bensen's question, which led to a discussion about the nature of customer service in general, which led them to a discussion of advertising. An hour later they were deep in conversation about the complicated relationship between collegiate athletics and the revenue generated by collegiate athletics, still seated in the same chairs, each sipping from a second glass of Caspian Sea Mr. Bensen had poured from bottles he kept in a nearby fridge. Derek finished his glass and said, "You know, I've been a Coke guy since I was a kid and I've only had Caspian Sea a couple times. But I've gotta tell you, it's pretty good stuff."

"Glad you like it. Buy it." Mr. Bensen glanced at the clock across the room. "Wow. Derek, it's been a good hour, but I'm afraid we've gotta wind things up." He stood up, and so did Derek, and they shook hands. Derek wasn't sure what to do. He was glad he'd gotten through the conversation without looking like an idiot, but he wasn't sure he'd accomplished anything. Besides his Chick-fil-A line, he didn't go into the meeting with any planned course of conversation or action, and he was starting to regret it.

He stopped before he left the office.

"Yeah, well, thanks for the drinks. Thanks for the time."

"My pleasure," said Mr. Bensen.

Derek missed the joke. "Mr. Bensen. I'm not sure—I appreciate your willingness to talk and all. Honestly, I feel like I maybe wasted your time though."

"Why's that?"

"What'd we talk about? Football?"

"Are you concerned about my time or yours? I chose to talk for the last hour. I'm fine with my time. What did you choose to do?"

"No, it's not that I expected anything in particular. But ... "

"Relax, seriously. You knew you had to come see me when I invited you to my office, even though you had no idea what to expect. But you did expect something, right? Be honest."

"Yeah, I guess."

"What?"

"I don't know. Maybe to learn something? I don't know."

"Okay. First of all, so much of what you will or won't do in business will come down to relationships—call it *networking* if you want—like your professor—but it's more than that. It's more than *who you know*. It's *who you are*. I don't know who you are, but I know more about you now than I did an hour ago. You *do* want something from me—something direct or specific, even if you can't tell me what it is. And I want something from you.

"For the last couple of months I've been thinking about starting a mentoring relationship with the college—you know I went there too? I'd like to find someone with talent and character who could use a break and who'd work hard once he or she got one."

"Uh, right," Derek answered. "So, you want to mentor me?"

"I don't know. You want to be mentored? I'm just kind of toying with the idea and I'd like to see how it could work and how it might benefit you and Caspian Sea."

Derek said nothing.

"Think about it. No pressure. If you're interested, call up when you can and tell Mrs. Howe you need to see me one hour each week—she'll figure out the details with you."

"Seriously?"

"Yeah. Can you work that into your schedule?"

"Yes sir," Derek said and smiled.

"Okay. There you go." They shook hands again. "Maybe next time you'll learn something," Mr. Bensen joked.

"Maybe so," Derek said and headed toward the elevator. He breathed easy once he was down on the ground floor and outside the building. He wasn't sure what he'd expected to accomplish or how he expected he would feel, but he was glad the first meeting with Mr. Bensen was over.

Derek was only a block away from Mr. Bensen's building, waiting behind other pedestrians to cross at a busy intersection, when he heard a strange voice directly behind him.

"Derek."

Derek turned and looked up at Stovall, who had barely noticeable beads of sweat above his lip. "Do I know you?"

"You do now."

"I'm sorry?"

"Walk," Stovall said as if he had a gun in Derek's back. Just as he said it, the red hand switched to the white stick figure and the entire group of waiting walkers began to cross the street. Derek stood still and looked over his shoulder at Stovall.

"Are you from Caspian Sea?"

"Wouldn't you just love that? You'd *love* that wouldn't you? Walk!"

IV

The night of the dinner, immediately after Bensen had told him about his new intern, Stovall called Toth to congratulate him on orchestrating a successful plan. It had been two weeks since their talk on the driving range and Toth and Stovall had not talked about the Caspian Sea formula since. Stovall had forgotten about the entire thing until he saw Bensen offer his card to a waiter at the dinner. He was impressed with Toth's ability to get things done and wanted to let him know.

Toth had also forgotten about the driving range conversation. He was more disturbed by Stovall's willingness to maintain a cordial relationship with Bensen than he was interested in illegally obtaining information from Caspian Sea with the intent of developing a competitive product. However, when Stovall called with his congratulations, Toth was not able to admit that he'd dropped the whole thing. Caught off guard at first, Toth quickly understood what had happened and took credit for finding a finance student who would volunteer at the banquet, work the head table, and engage Bensen in conversation enough to be offered an internship. Stovall was impressed with what he thought was Toth's brilliance.

As soon as the phone conversation ended, Toth went to work to figure out how he could work this situation to accomplish what he'd only whimsically suggested on the driving range two weeks before.

Two days later, Toth called Stovall.

"Sean. You ready for some action?"

"Always," Stovall replied.

"Okay. We're moving into the next phase with the intern."

"Bring it."

"Listen. The kid doesn't know you—doesn't know anything about you, right?"

"Right."

"Okay. All I told him is that he needed to get himself in position to be asked to be an intern and we'd ask him for some information and pay him well if he got it. The kid's good at what he does, obviously."

"Yeah, I'm telling ya, I watched him all night—he looked all nervous and sheepish—pretty pathetic."

"Yeah, I told him that angle would probably work—he's good. But here's the thing—I don't wanna pay the kid cash—not cash in hand anyway. If he's a loose cannon or something and decides to go off on his own with the information or whatever, then we don't have anything on him. But, if he's on your payroll, then we've got more control over him and there's no way to trace that he's working on this illegal thing for us—if he starts talking, he's just a crazy guy with a grudge against management and you fire him and no one listens to him anymore."

"You think he's that kind of kid? Like he'd try that on us? On you?"

"He's a kid who's willing to do something illegal for money—how can you trust a kid like that?"

"Okay. Fine. So what's the action?"

"You'll like this. You're gonna be like the muscle goon who's made money and is now calling the shots—mafia kind of stuff. You're in charge, but you're way too emotional to make good decisions. You scare everyone to death, so most people listen to you. You find this kid *after* his first meeting with Bensen—like right after, but it's gotta be *after*. You find him, approach him and get him to sit down with you on a bench or at a coffee shop or something and you tell him. *I know you're working for Bensen. I'll double it.* He'll say something. No matter what he says you say, *I'll triple it.* He'll ask you who you are and you say, *Don't you worry your pretty little head about that.*"

"Pretty little head?"

"You're trying to scare him. *Don't worry your pretty little head.* This is you talking to him. And you keep going, *Here's what you need to know. I'll triple what he's paying you and I'll bust your kneecaps if*

*you say anything to him or anyone else about it. Think about it if you
need to. I'll see you soon.* Something like that. That's it."

"I don't know if I like it, man. It's weird. Threatening a kid in a
coffee shop? Why?"

"Trust me Sean, I've got the whole thing worked out. It's not good
to know too much. You know Woody Allen only gives his actors their
own lines? They don't see anything else. It makes it real. That's what
I'm working on with you and this kid. Trust me—it's necessary."

"Woody Allen? Where do you get all this stuff? You need a
girlfriend."

"You got your part?" Toth asked.

"I got it."

V

Derek walked and Stovall followed. Derek had no idea what was
going on. Neither did Stovall. When they reached the opposite sidewalk, Stovall stepped half in front of Derek and said, "Have a seat."

Derek stopped walking, swallowed hard, and asked, "Where?"
There were no benches or tables. Other pedestrians weaved around
the two of them standing in the middle of the sidewalk.

"Here, move over to the wall," Stovall said. They both awkwardly
shifted a few feet toward the wall of the nearest building.

"What's going on?" Derek asked.

"I'm looking for a park bench." Stovall glanced around in all
directions.

"There's a park just up there—one more block."

"Good. Okay. Go."

Stovall and Derek walked together, both looking rather confused.
Derek looked scared as well. Stovall was nervous. He tried to remember his lines. They stepped into the small park and sat at the first iron
bench they found.

"Okay kid. Listen. I'll pay you double whatever he's paying you."

"What?" Derek squinted into the sun shining through tree leaves.

"I'll pay you double."

"Double what?"

"Whatever he's paying you."

"I'm not getting paid anything. Are you a Caspian Sea employee? Seriously, I'm just a student. Mr. Bensen's working on an internship program and he wanted to ask me some questions."

"Triple. I'll triple it. Final offer. Take it or leave it." Stovall looked around nervously at the dog-walkers and stroller-pushers moving through his vision.

"But what's the offer? Three times zero is zero." Derek didn't know what else to say.

Stovall had no idea what to do or say next. He almost spat when he leaned in and whispered into Derek's face, "I'll kneecap your pretty little head!" Derek's head jolted back. Stovall swallowed hard. His face went pale.

"Are you okay?" Derek asked.

"Listen. I'm sorry, I'm no good at this. I'm the other guy."

"What other guy?"

"Toth told me he didn't tell you about me, but he had to. Even if he didn't, I'm the other guy who's part of the plan. It was kind of my plan to begin with and then it got all crazy for some reason because Toth wants you to work for me—which is fine with me—so that's what needs to happen. You need to work for me. I don't know. I'm sure I've messed something up now, by telling you that. Woody Allen wouldn't like it. Not sure what. Anyway, Toth'll get in touch with you soon, I assume, and tell you the next step. Listen. I'm sorry. Really. I'm just no good at this kind of thing. You're good, though. I was watching you the other night—you were great—very impressive. Good work. Anyway, I'm sure I'll see you again. Keep up the good work and you'll be paid well—handsomely." Stovall stood and extended his hand to Derek.

Derek shook it and remained seated on the bench and squinted, watching Stovall walk away. When Stovall rounded the corner of the block and was out of sight, Derek reached for his phone. He stared at the screen. He didn't know who to call or what exactly to say. He stared through his phone at the sidewalk in front of him, frozen.

Suddenly, he was in shade. Two shiny black shoes stopped toe to toe in front of his boots. He prayed they didn't belong to the man who'd just walked away. They did't. They were Toth's.

VI

Toth's frame put Derek entirely in shadow. He was glad to be able to stand in the open. He'd been ducking and hiding all afternoon, watching Stovall clumsily stalk and confront Derek. He was not as large as Stovall, but he knew the impression he'd create if he was eclipsing the sun the first time Derek saw him. "Who you gonna call there, chief?" he asked.

Derek looked up at Toth's silhouette—black suit, white shirt, no tie, aviator shades. Derek said nothing.

"From now on, you call me. I'm Steve Moss." Toth extended his hand. Derek, perplexed, shook it gingerly and then gripped it tighter when Toth pulled on it to help him stand up. "Let's walk."

As they walked slowly through the park, Toth (as Moss) explained that he was a government agent. He said they'd been following leads on a huge fraud case for years that had recently led them to Bensen and Stovall. They knew they were close to something—he was close to something—and so did Stovall and Bensen. Moss explained how Bensen's strategy had been to appear as more of a philanthropist to look less suspicious to the feds. Stovall wasn't as smart. He seemed to have no strategy besides paranoia.

"Stovall's gonna crack any day—he's been on medication for years, but it's not enough to help him deal with our heat. We just hope he lasts long enough to lead us to what we need. That's where you come in. What did he do there? What did he say? Did he offer you a job?"

"That guy? Back there? Man, I don't know. He was nuts. Who's Toth?"

"Toth? He mentioned Toth? Forget Toth. Did he offer you a position in his company?"

"He told me he'd triple my pay, but I'm not getting paid anything."

"Okay, fine. He's offering to get you into his company to keep you away from Bensen. Take the offer."

"I'm in school. I don't have time to work full time."

"He's not asking you to work at all. He's offering to put you on his payroll to keep you away from Caspian Sea. Who knows what he's trying to gain or hide? The thing is, if you do what he wants, you give us a valuable man on the inside. Also, if he gets what he wants, maybe he'll relax a little and we'll buy some time before he totally melts down. We need him to stay healthy and keep working. Also, you get some real cash. Triple whatever you're getting now."

"I'm getting nothing now. Three times zero is zero."

Moss stopped and so did Derek. Moss leaned in and whispered through moist lips and coffee breath into Derek's face. "Listen. Don't get all *college* on me, boy. You want me to leave you hanging out to dry on this? I will. You want that lunatic following you around, accosting you between classes, following you to the can, jumping out of closets at frat parties? You wanna deal with that yourself? Don't play *I'm smarter than you* with me."

"I was just saying … "

Moss held up a fist with one finger sticking out in front of Derek's face. "Think."

"Okay. Tell me what to do." They started walking again and Moss explained to Derek how he could get on Stovall's payroll without having to meet Stovall again. Derek was happy to hear that. "So wh then?"

"Just be a student and do your thing. My hunch is Stovall won't need you to do much. If he does, it's better for us—you'll be able to get in and do some research."

"What about Mr. Bensen?"

"*Mr.* Bensen. Your *mentor*," Moss said and spat in the grass. "You like him don't you?"

"He seems like a good guy."

"Oh, he's good alright. But what's he good *at*, exactly? That's what we want to know. You get me?"

"Not really."

"There are two big things you need to do with Bensen, and they should be easy because he's really trying hard at this do-gooder routine. Number one, meet with him regularly and don't let on that you know anything about the investigation. He's dangerous—more dangerous than Stovall—but he won't act on anything unless he's personally threatened and there's no way he'll feel threatened by you if you just play the good college boy. He sees you as part of his solution, not part of his problem. Just keep it that way. Number two, get the formula for the drink."

"Isn't it on the can?"

"No. That's all corn syrup and calories. He's got his own herbs-and-spices mystery going on and ... " Moss grimaced dramatically. "Listen, I can't tell you exactly why this matters, but it does. Let's leave it at that. If you get that formula, you've done some real good for national security—the world. I'll say that. *And*, you'll get a pay-\
~ck that'll be much bigger than triple what you're getting now."

\
~k barely opened his mouth to talk, thought better of it, and \
ead. After a few steps he said, "This is wild. Can I say no? \
: to go back to being an average student?"

\
:. You've got freedom. I exist to protect that freedom. \
ise of some choices you've already made, you've also \
ned Stovall barking up your tree. That's real. That's \
: threaten you?"

"He told me he'd kneecap my pretty little head."

Moss puffed out a tiny chuckle, then tried to turn it into a cough.

"Yeah," Derek grinned. "I don't even know what that means."

Moss recovered himself, stopped walking, and clenched his jaw and his fists. Derek stopped too and took a step back toward Moss, who leaned in and whispered in Derek's face again, "Son, you don't want to find out. Trust me." He pulled a card out of his shirt pocket with two fingers and handed it to Derek. "Think about it, but not for long. When you've made a decision, call me. Anything happens, you think of anything, you wonder about anything—anything at all—you call me." Moss slapped Derek on the upper arm, turned, and vanished around the nearest corner. Derek, still with his phone in his hand, put it back into his pocket and kept walking.

VII

The following Wednesday, Derek was back in the elevator. As he rose and looked out over the sea of suits, he thought differently about them. He wondered which suit was Moss. He wondered which suit was Stovall. He hoped none of them. He'd called Stovall's company, visited the Human Resources office, signed forms, and was told his first check would be deposited in his account in two weeks. He had no idea how much money that would be. He didn't dare tell anyone ever again that three times zero equaled zero. He had talked to no one about Stovall or Bensen or Moss. He told a couple of friends he was doing an internship downtown—that was all.

After setting things up with Stovall Enterprises, he had called Moss. His head had cleared a bit after the initial encounters with both Moss and Stovall, and he remembered that Stovall had talked about a man named Toth and he'd talked about some kind of plan. Derek told Moss about this. He was concerned that this *Toth guy* or Stovall would come looking for him, especially if he went to meet Mr. Bensen. Moss told

Derek he had *guys* all over both Toth and Stovall and they wouldn't let either man get near Derek. Moss told him to relax, stay smart, make his next Bensen meeting, and stay in touch.

The elevator stopped and Derek turned to walk through the door. He'd been comfortable in Mr. Bensen's office before and he felt comfortable again, in spite of all he'd heard from Moss and Stovall. Mrs. Howe seemed to recognize him when he arrived at the office. "Good afternoon," she smiled, "Go on in."

Derek walked in and Mr. Bensen stood and walked out from behind his desk with his hand outstretched. "Alright, who's ready to learn?" Mr. Bensen smiled.

They shook hands and Derek chuckled and said, "Hello."

"You've brought a notebook. Well done. Have a seat. Let's get to business." Derek sat in the same chair he'd sat in the week before. Mr. Bensen went to the fridge and pulled out two glasses with ice in them and two bottles of Caspian Sea and filled the glasses. He brought them to the table and placed them on Caspian Sea coasters.

"Thanks," Derek said, and took a drink. "Okay. What's the secret?"

"The secret? Hah. You wanna know what's in the drink?"

Derek felt the blood in his face heat up. He hadn't decided what he should do about the secret formula—if he should ever ask, if he should ask early or give it a few weeks, if he should see what he was getting paid first—the only thing he was sure of is he wanted to look and sound like a student. He was a student. A student would ask a successful businessman, *What's the secret of running a successful business?* That's what Derek thought he was asking. Instead he'd gotten straight to a place he wasn't sure he ever wanted to be. His face still hot, he asked, "You'd tell me?"

"Ice," Bensen said.

Derek stared blankly for a second, then grinned. Mr. Bensen chuckled. Derek relaxed a bit. "Of course. Gotcha—you got me, I guess. No, what's the secret of running a successful business?" Derek asked.

Mr. Bensen smiled and shook his head. "A secret," he said. "Do you want to solve a mystery or get rich quick?"

Derek looked confused and said nothing.

"You don't know the answer to a question so you're calling it a *secret*. But if you treat it like a secret then you turn it into something it's not. What's your real question?"

Derek thought and looked out at the surrounding buildings of the city while Mr. Bensen sipped his drink and waited. He wasn't sure what Mr. Bensen wanted to know. He wasn't sure of much.

"I don't know. It's all complicated."

"Why?"

"Okay. Maybe it isn't." Derek tried his hardest to think and act like a student instead of a spy. "What are some basic elements—what's the most basic element of running a successful company?" Derek asked.

"Money," Mr. Bensen answered. "You have to make money. That answer is simple. All corporations are essentially the same. They need to raise money as cheaply as possible and use it as efficiently as possible to make a product that customers will pay a lot of money for. There's a lot of uncertainty and risk—some things you can see coming and prepare for, some just explode out of nowhere—I've had to make hundreds of tough judgment calls. Some situations come up repeatedly and you learn from what you've done before, but a lot of it is just learning as you go—building instincts."

"But how do you build instincts?" Derek asked, "I thought you're born with instincts."

"You're born with some instincts, but you need to build others to survive or succeed in different environments. Most people duck when a baseball is hit at them. Those who don't have trained themselves to watch a ball come off a bat, identify where it's going, then try to get in the way of it to stop it or catch it. An accomplished infielder does this over and over; it becomes instinct and he gets in front of every ball hit his way. But when he was six years old, he would've run away crying if balls were repeatedly hit at him."

"So experience builds instincts?"

"Experience helps, but the key is learning the fundamentals and repeatedly rehearsing them so you get comfortable with the process and familiar with the task. Fielding ground balls, playing scales on a piano, baking cakes, whatever."

"Doing homework, creating *Balance Sheets*," Derek added.

"Yup. But even before that, it's basic math—what is it? x = y? Algebra. All that stuff. That wasn't even college—that was high school. That's you starting to build your instincts. Algebra, a little logic, a little Psychology—that's all there is to Finance. Luck—there's luck too. No professors for that though, huh?"

"Judgment calls—you mentioned judgment calls," Derek said. "What are some of those?"

"Yeah, wow, every day there's a new one, really," Mr. Bensen said. "The whole thing started with a judgment call."

"Tell me about that—about the beginning."

"The beginning? Of the whole thing?" Mr. Bensen asked.

"Yeah."

"Wow. Okay." Mr. Bensen took a drink from his glass and put it back on the table and leaned back in his chair. "It was the first week of summer after my junior year of college—right after finals. I was invited to spend the week on a lake in the mountains with a few guys. My roommate at the time had grown up with this kid, Spencer Wells, whose family owned a lake house. I was ready to get home for the summer and make some money mowing yards, but I heard Spencer's family was loaded; they had boats and jet skis and his parents had stocked the place with food and drinks, though—and this is key—no alcohol. Spencer's mother was—still is—an executive with JP Morgan and his father was a state trooper. Not much illegal happening around that family.

"So I went along. Turns out, about twenty people found their way through the mountains to Spencer's place—they'd planned for six or seven. Twenty college kids in the mountains, no fast food for miles—every consumable thing in the house was gone by the second day. These were the days before ATMs, when banks only cashed checks for their customers and stores only accepted local checks— especially little mountain stores. Spencer called his parents and they weren't happy. They agreed with the owner of the local store—about a 30-minute drive from the house—to allow Spencer to buy some stuff on credit. But they restricted what he could get, to mostly bread and meat and water. A few folks left, but most of us stuck around and lived on sandwiches. Everyone got tired of drinking water fast.

"But there was this kid, Alex Romero, who was—still is—a bit nuts. He didn't really seem to be connected to anyone else there. He was a Chemistry major and had just developed a health drink for a final project. Alex talked to Spencer about his concoction and ended up talking to Spencer's parents on the phone to persuade them to let us buy the ingredients he needed to make it. It would, he assured them, keep us all hydrated betetr than water. They agreed and we took another trip to the store and came back with boxes of fruit and all kinds of other stuff. Alex locked himself in the kitchen and came out an hour or so later with a couple of pitchers of the best lemonade/juice/drink stuff you've ever had."

"Lemonade?" Derek asked.

"It was like lemonade, but it had this extra thing going on that wasn't sour but wasn't too sweet—Alex tried to keep the plum part secret as long as possible."

Derek wrote down the word 'plum.' He wondered if that was enough to satisfy Moss. But, as he listened, he realized there must be more.

"Everyone wanted more so he went back in and went to work. People offered but he didn't want any help. He'd lock the door, and come out with batch after batch of the stuff. There were jokes about what was in it, but after a glass of it, no one cared as long as Alex kept making it. He became a sensation. He was a hero. Everyone was all over him with hugs and laughs and pats on the back. I think people were genuinely touched and felt guilty because he was making this fantastic drink and everyone was loving it but he wasn't getting anything out of it. The girls who were there had barely noticed him before, but they were suddenly looking for him all the time. I told him he should charge by the glass or the pitcher or something and we started talking.

"I was blown away by how good the drink was, and by how magical it seemed. I went home and worked on yards all summer. I found myself craving it regularly. When everyone came back to school in late August it was still warm and people were filling the quad and fields around campus playing pick-up games, running, riding bikes, and hanging out. I wanted more of the drink and I thought it was worth seeing if others were willing to pay for it. I found Alex and it didn't take much to convince him that it was worth a shot. He didn't know anything about making money. I didn't know much. I was a Finance major but I was a distracted student. I didn't pay attention until I thought I really needed to know information. I suddenly started realizing I needed to know lots of things I'd missed in classes. We went shopping with my credit card. We picked up plums and lemons and oranges and all the other stuff and bought a big cooler, a ladle, and some cups. We took it to my place—my kitchen was way cleaner than Alex's—he went to work and produced a cooler full of the drink. I took a couple sips. I told him it was good, but didn't tell him that it wasn't as good as the stuff we'd had in the mountains. Honestly, the stuff he put together that week was better than anything we've been able to come up with since.

"We threw a card table and the drink and stuff in my car, drove to campus and found a big tree in the middle of the action and set up a stand. We hadn't come up with a name, so we just wrote *lemonade 50 cents* on a sign and hung it off the side of the table. In an hour we had $50 and an empty cooler and a line of thirsty and disappointed people who wanted more."

"When did you stop calling it lemonade?"

"Pretty early. It got to be frustrating talking to people under the tree who kept telling us it wasn't lemonade. Alex was a little protective of the plum secret, but we told a few folks and started asking people for name suggestions. One guy said, 'How about Plum Island?' I sort of nodded and he walked way—never saw him again."

"Plum Island?" Derek asked.

"Yeah, that's what we were calling it for a long time. I still slip up and call it that once in a while."

"So what happened?"

"We found out there's a couple of real Plum Islands. One in Lake Michigan, one off the coast of Connecticut. The one off Connecticut is the home of the Plum Island Animal Disease Center—not great to have your refreshing drink linked in any way to the word disease. So we did some looking around and found out that plums are thought to have originated in the Caucasus Mountains off the Caspian Sea."

"There you go."

"Yup. But, we were Plum Island for a while. So, we were under the tree regularly and we had a name, but we had one big problem: cash flow. I'd paid enough attention in class to know that was a problem. We wanted to stay simple. All we needed was a stainless steel cart with wheels. We'd fill it with ice and the drink and sell medium, large, and extra-large cups' full. But all that took money, and we didn't have any. So, we bought what we needed and I put everything on my credit card—not that smart, but what else could we do? The cart and the cooler were one-time expenses, but every Friday we'd go buy all the ingredients and make the stuff. Saturday morning we'd buy ice and be under the tree by 11:00. By 3:00 pm we'd sell the last cup and go home with a big pot of money—a jar actually, a big 2-gallon pickle jar. We had some cash, but we weren't sure what to do with it. Should we use the money to pay off the credit card? Should we just pay back what we spent on fruit or pay off the cart? Or should we use some of the money to buy more ingredients for next week? We could sell more, but my credit card was maxed out after buying the cart and a few weekends' worth of ingredients; our purchase power was limited severely. So we saved enough to pay for the ingredients, but we didn't pay a dime toward the cart. We just paid back the amount for the ingredients plus the interest on the cart. That was a problem. The interest rate on the credit card was ridiculous—29.99%.

"By October the warm weather was gone and so were our sales. We quit for the year and planned to open up as early as possible in the spring. That winter was full of bad business news. First, I couldn't keep up the credit card payments without income. The cart was sitting in storage at my apartment—I was trying to pay it off without the help of the money it was supposed to be bringing in. Money was going out but none was coming in. I didn't need classes to know that wouldn't end well. Second, we found out that we had been operating illegally. Justin Pearson, a law student with big legal and financial aspirations who'd become a regular customer, ran into me one day on campus and asked a few questions about licensing and taxes. He broke it to me that we'd been breaking more than a few laws. The only good news is that we had a good idea."

"So was this guy threatening you with legal action?" Derek asked. He'd written down the name "Justin Pearson."

"No—nothing like that. He wanted to make sure he could still drink Plum Island when we started up again. He also wanted to make some money off of helping us get legal, but we had no money to pay him. He wasn't a lawyer yet anyway, so he made us an offer. He'd find us an attorney and basically pay what it would cost to get us legal. I offered him a chance to own part of the company but he didn't want that. It took him a few months, but the following Spring he wrote us a check for $10,000—not sure where a law student got that kind of cash, but he had it. That paid his lawyer buddy. In return, we paid him $11,000 the following year. I think he put that toward a Jaguar when he finished law school. He's probably bought a Jaguar every year since then."

"So that got you legal?" Derek asked as he circled "Justin Pearson" and wrote dollar signs by his name.

"Yes, but we were still stuck. We needed cash to pay off the cart so we could use our credit cards to buy ingredients to make more lemonade in the spring.

"We went back to Spencer Wells—the guy with the lake house. All we had to do was convince him to let us have some cash—Alex had actually already done that on a small scale in the summer with his parents. Here's where it gets interesting.

"The bad thing about the winter was we had no income. The good thing was we had time. We knew we had a product that would sell and we started really thinking big. That's when we started researching the name and changed it. I also did some corporate research and found out that businesses could be sole proprietorships, partnerships, or corporations. There is also a hybrid of those called a limited liability company—LLC—that's what we went with—Caspian Sea Drinks, LLC. We also talked a lot about how we could get bigger. We thought about all kinds of things from selling coffee and hot chocolate from the cart in the winter, to making brownies or hot dogs. But we decided to stick with the drink, just make it bigger. It was a big enough school and there were thirsty people with money in their pockets all over campus, all day long, who may never walk by our tree. There were also thirsty people all over town and all across the state—all across the country. Why not try to get Caspian Sea all the way to both Plum Islands and everywhere else in the US?"

"Why stop there? Why not to the Caspian Sea? Why not the world?"

"I wasn't thinking on the Coke level—not then. I crunched numbers and knew it was big, but I came up with the number we needed to pay off my card and get started doing serious business: $140,000. Like I started to say before, we'd gotten help from Spencer Wells before, at the lake house. We figured we'd try him out again. It was quick. We met, told him our plan, told him we were legal, told him what we needed, and asked him to talk to his parents. He got back to us the next day and agreed to put up $40,000, but he wanted to own 50% of the company. I told him he watched too many movies. After some relatively soft negotiations, we settled on him owning 30% and Alex and I each owning 35%. You with me?"

"Yup. You still need $100,000."

"Right. Sean Stovall," Mr. Bensen said. He noticed something on Derek's face when he said the name. "You know him?"

"No. Who? Never heard of him. Who?" Derek replied. He didn't write anything in his notebook.

"Sean Stovall. He's a pretty legitimate guy now—still in town. Back then he wasn't much but a trust-fund brat. This is a great story. So I'm at a baseball game with Spencer—his mom sometimes got company seats up the first base line—great seats. Spencer knew Stovall casually—I'd never seen him before. He was sitting behind us, drinking constantly, making bets on where the ball would end up between innings—on the mound, or on the grass. You know, an outfielder catches a fly ball for the third out, then runs in to his dugout and tosses the ball toward the mound. They were betting on whether it'd end up on the mound or roll off in the dirt—the loser bought the next beer. Stovall lost every time through the sixth inning. He'd had way too much to drink and he was angry. He started putting money on it instead of beer—$20. He won the first time. Then he wanted to make it $50. His buddy told him he was crazy. Stovall stood up holding a $50 bill trying to get someone to bet him for the next inning. He was explaining the game to fathers and kids and old ladies with scorebooks sitting around him. Embarrassing. We ended up on a bus with him after the game and I asked him where his money came from. He had no problem telling me how loaded his family was and how loaded his fiancée's family was. He had no problem telling me he'd been given $100,000 the week before by a future uncle-in-law, but how it was useless because the uncle was going to make him invest it. He said no one in his family trusted him with large sums of money and he was stressed out because he'd promised his fiancée a Wimbledon honeymoon the following summer. He had some money set aside, but he still needed $8,000 to cover the trip. I said to him, 'I own a company. You give me that $100,000 tomorrow—invest it in my company—and I'll give you $108,000 in time for your honeymoon.' He squinted a little, and then stuck out his hand and we shook on it. I was shocked when he showed up the next afternoon, fully sober, wrote a check to Caspian Sea, and signed a contract with us. Spencer couldn't believe it."

"*I* don't believe it."

"Luck. There's a good deal of luck involved. Luck and paying attention." Mr. Bensen stood up, walked over to the windows, and looked out. "We started out as two guys with a Visa card. Then we got Justin and Spencer to put in some money and got crazy lucky with Stovall. Then came the angel investors, then the Chick-fil-A account, then more trouble, then venture capitalists, then going public with JP Morgan, then Coke. I know it all happened, but it's hard to think about how."

"Venture capitalists? Angel investors? Chick-fil-A again? You did quite a fast-forward there."

"I know. When we went public, life changed," Mr. Bensen said and turned back around and headed back to the table.

"But what happened between finding those first investors and being bought by Coke?"

"A whole lot. But I'm gonna jump around a little to explain some important concepts. It'll make sense."

Derek looked a little confused.

"Relax. Listen." Mr. Bensen continued. "Go back to when Alex, Spencer, and I were the owners. Alex and I were having fun. We enjoyed the work, but we were in it to make money. We did all the work. Spencer was a passive investor. He invested his $40,000 for one reason—to make money. Times were pretty simple then. We pretty much agreed on everything. Why not? Anything that was good for me was good for those guys too. We all knew exactly what was going on. We could have an owners' meeting in the back of a cab. When we went public all that changed. We gained thousands of *owners*. Pension funds, mutual funds, hedge funds, little old ladies, and day traders—anyone can own a share of Caspian Sea. All these owners have the same goal, which is the same as our goal: to make money. Technically, they want us to maximize shareholder wealth. But with a big company like that, maximizing shareholder wealth isn't always the same as maximizing my wealth—management's wealth.

"They have one big problem: information—the lack of information. Legally, we are required to disclose financial statements. We release an *Income Statement, Balance Sheet,* and *Statement of Cash Flows.* You know anything about those?" Mr. Bensen asked. Derek didn't answer quickly enough. "You need to know that stuff. Those things are important. Here's one reason.

"Ten months after Justin and Stovall loaned us money we thought things were going great, but we were burning cash. According to our arrangement, in two months we were going to have to pay Justin that $10,000 plus $1,000 interest. We also owed Stovall $108,000. We had $33,000 in cash. The contracts with those guys were clear. If we didn't pay them, they got our business. No way were we gonna let that happen. Over a year of serious energy wasted? We needed $119,000 in two months or it was over."

"So the jam you were in earlier in the winter before Stovall gave you that $100,000—that was nothing compared to $119,000 in two months." Derek wrote down '$119,000/2 months. How???'

"Tell me about it. It was imminent doom. We had no idea what to do. I laid out the full situation to Alex and Spencer one afternoon sitting around the living room. We all just stared at the floor. It was tough. I had talked Spencer into putting $40,000 of his inheritance into Caspian Sea and if we didn't turn $33,000 into $119,000 in two months, he would lose it all. I'd let him down. That was worse than the thought of losing my own money. After a few minutes of silence Alex stood up and said, 'Vegas. Let's go.'"

"Ha," Derek chuckled.

"What? He was serious. It took me the rest of the afternoon to convince both him and Spencer that gambling was not our solution. Those were a few genuinely dark days. I knew Vegas wasn't an option, but it started to sound viable after a few days of having no alternative. Then I got an excited call from Spencer. He told me he'd made us an appointment to meet with a woman his mom knew—a lady named Natasha who ran a thing called the Angel Investors Network. Sounded good to me. I'd never heard of angel investors but I'd been doing some major praying. It turns out they weren't anything too magical.

"Angel investors are people with some extra cash who want to make more, and are looking to invest in the next big thing—doctors, lawyers, and professional athletes who know they need to invest but don't want to go the conventional route. Natasha worked for them screening new businesses. She'd give owners a shot at pitching to her and, if she liked them, she'd give them a chance to pitch to her group of investors. Spencer's mom had talked to her and she agreed to meet us in a couple of days. I had a few gray T-shirts made up with a logo I'd come up with—a purple plum with a bendy straw sticking out of it. Alex and I wore the T-shirts with jeans to the meeting with Natasha at her office downtown—just a few blocks from here actually—and I brought along a shirt for her too. We felt a little odd walking through the lobby of her building carrying a cooler and some plastic cups and a T-shirt, but we were confident in the drink and in our ability to sell it.

"The confidence vanished when we walked into Natasha's office. Spencer told us she was young, but that's all we knew. Turns out, she was a former Olympic swimmer, extremely attractive and extremely intense. She hit the intercom button on the phone as soon as we walked in and asked the lady at the front desk why two boys in

T-shirts were in her office. She then called Spencer's mom and asked her if she knew us—staring at us the whole time. She was clearly upset, referred to us again as boys, then listened for a few minutes and hung up the phone.

"She asked us, 'Why are you here?' I was terrified. I said something about needing funding for Caspian Sea. She fired back with a series of questions. 'Why do you need funding? If your product is any good why isn't it making you money? Why don't you put your own money in? Why won't someone else fund you? Why are you coming to me?'

"I thought I had a good answer. 'Sales are great. We already put in all the money we have and we owe two of our investors—'

"'You have investors but you can't manage cash flows. Where are the financial statements?'

"I didn't know what to say. Alex decided to talk, 'We thought if you tried the drink—' She stood up—business suit, skirt, long swimming legs, high heels—and walked around her desk, right between Alex and me, opened the door and said to the ceiling as if she couldn't bear to look at us, 'Take your picnic to a park. Come back in one week, dressed, and with financials.' She waited for two seconds while we stood not knowing what to do. 'One week! Go.'"

"Wow!" Derek laughed.

"Yeah, we felt like idiots. Spencer called me before I could call him. His mom had torn him apart on the phone, and then he laid into me. Alex ended up apologizing to Spencer's mom, agreed that we were silly kids and convinced her to beg for another shot. That night we had dinner with her. She sat us down and lectured us first, then gave us a run-down of all we needed to have for the Natasha meeting the following week. She was spoon-feeding us, which wasn't like her, but her relationship with Natasha had already been jeopardized and she wanted to be sure to mend it as quickly as possible. Again, so much in this business is about relationships and trust. So, she taught us and we took heavy notes and worked like crazy over the next few days. A week later we were back at Natasha's office in borrowed suits, though I did wear my plum t-shirt under my dress shirt.

"We sat in chairs facing her desk, swallowing and sweating like crazy through the whole meeting. She was all business—didn't acknowledge that she'd ever seen us before. Alex didn't say a word. I presented the financials I'd learned backwards and forwards. I had answers for all her questions. After what felt like forever but was only about twelve minutes, she put her hands on her desk like she was about to stand up and said, 'Sophie coached you boys. She's smart, eh?' 'She sure is,' I said, not sure if we'd cheated or not. 'Where is the drink?' she asked. Alex and I looked at each other, blank. 'It's okay. Next time bring the drink. There is a group coming here in two weeks. You will do all of this again for them. Everything like today, I will ask the same questions, they won't say much. For them, bring the drink—make cups with that purple thing on the side. We will see.' She stood and we stood. I thought she might walk around the desk to shake our hands or something. 'Two weeks! Go.'

"We met with Spencer's mom that night and told her how it all went. She was relieved and told us we'd done great. All I had to do in those two weeks was get fifteen Caspian Sea cups made up. When we went back to Natasha's office with the cooler and the cups, it was just like she said it would be. She asked questions, the investors said only a few things, they tasted the drink (Natasha never touched it), they loved it, they all stood up and shook hands with us, and we left. Natasha called that night and told us ten investors committed $100,000 each—we had a million dollars."

"Whoa! A million dollars? Just like that? In one shot?"

"One shot? We'd been selling the drink for two years—we put in countless hours in those two weeks before the meeting, not to mention all the hours before that. The meeting was the tip of the iceberg."

"Yeah, but a million dollars."

"Alex thought the same thing. He thought he was a millionaire. I'd matured enough and knew enough at that point to simply be excited about paying off our other investors and staying in business. It took me quite a while to explain to him that it'd still be a while before we could spend a dime on ourselves."

"Why's that? Why couldn't you spend any of it?" Derek asked.

"We could spend it, but only on the business. We wouldn't benefit from investment money until we were able to afford salaries for ourselves, and even then, those salaries would have to be modest. We had to grow before we could do enough business to make real profits. All the numbers made Alex's head spin and he was frustrated. He was more frustrated when I explained to him that he'd have to stop making batches of the drink and come up with a formula that could be used to manufacture and bottle gallons and gallons of it. At least it was something he knew he could do. When we got the million, I officially became CEO of Caspian Sea Drinks. I appointed Alex President of Research and Development. After paying off Justin and Stovall, we started leasing warehouse space and bought all the equipment necessary to produce, bottle, and distribute bottles and cans of Caspian Sea."

"So you weren't under the tree anymore?"

"Nope. We did keep a couple of carts on campus, but we were focused on getting bottles of Caspian Sea in the juice section of local grocery stores and in the coolers in coffee shops and restaurants around town. We were officially in business, but we were still pretty small. We each had a small windowless office in the warehouse, but we went home to our little apartments we'd been renting for the last few years."

"So how much time passed between you setting up under the tree and you moving into the warehouse?"

"Two years."

"Is that fast? Slow? Average?"

"Depends on who you're talking to. It was fast enough for us. We were focused on local stuff and doing well and I didn't think we were ready for anything more than that. But then we got a call from Chick-fil-A."

"Chick-fil-A?"

"Yeah. All they said was that they wanted to talk to us about Caspian Sea. We prepared for the meeting like we'd prepared for the Natasha meeting—the second one—suits and all. But when we got there it was the exact opposite experience. The Vice President we met with was much more personable. She was a few years older than us, but she'd graduated from the college and we talked and realized we had several friends in common. We didn't have to do any convincing. She wanted to know if we'd be willing and able to let them include Caspian Sea in a couple of their stores. Chick-fil-A was growing and they wanted to continue growing, while maintaining a mom-and-pop reputation, as well as offering healthy food options. They thought Caspian Sea tasted good, but they also liked that we were virtually unknown. They'd love to take credit for discovering us. We were fine with all of it and worked out a simple distribution plan for those two store locations.

"We knew we'd be a hit at Chick-fil-A and that was good news and bad news at the same time. If we were a hit they'd want us to supply all their stores—good. In order to supply all their stores we'd have to ramp up production fast—bad. I worked up some projections of how things might go if Chick-fil-A wanted to use us nationally. We'd have markets in several different states. We'd need to either transport the drink from our one facility to all those towns in all those states, or we'd have to have other warehouses where we'd produce the drink. We would need a ton of money to maintain everything if it took off. We knew it would soon be time for the next step in acquiring financing—venture capitalists. You ever see *Wall Street*? Michael Douglas?"

"What's that? A TV show?"

"That's *Wall Street Week*—not on anymore. The movie, *Wall Street*. You haven't seen it? Every business major should watch that. Michael Douglas, Charlie Sheen. Finance in the 80s. Great stuff."

Derek wrote down *Charlie Sheen. Wall Street.* "I'll look for it," he said.

"Anyway, Gordon Gekko is this cut-throat huge money guy played by Michael Douglas. I knew we needed a meeting with guys like him, but I was scared to death thinking about it and had no idea how to make it happen. I called Spencer's mom. In the past, Alex was the one who talked to her and sort of begged her to make personal concessions for us—with the fruit and stuff for the drink at the lake house, with the second meeting with Natasha. But things were moving away from personal and closer to business. She still didn't stand to benefit much from us financially, but she would in the next step and a relationship with us was becoming as important for her as it was for us. She made some phone calls and got me in touch with the head of a venture capitalist firm in New York—the big boys. I did okay on the phone—we exchanged some information through the mail and scheduled a meeting a month later at their office in New York.

"Alex demanded that Caspian Sea cover all our expenses for the New York trip. He was happy to hear that the CEO was in full support of that. We booked a direct flight (I did have to talk Alex out of first class) and a suite in a nice hotel in Manhattan, and we flew up a couple days early specifically so we could do some suit shopping. We couldn't take any chances.

"The meeting went really well. The Natasha meetings and talks with Spencer's mom and the talks with Courtney at Chick-fil-A prepared both Alex and me for dealing with financial people, their questions and their lingo. We were on the 33rd floor of a building a couple blocks off Wall Street, down in the financial district. The location itself was intimidating, but the men and women in the room weren't all that different from Natasha and some of her angel investors—at least not in the way they presented themselves. There were six of them and they all worked for the firm—they worked for the Gordon Gekko's. They asked questions, we gave answers, they took notes, and the whole thing was over in about twenty-five minutes. The meeting was on a Friday morning. They knew we were staying in town for a few more days and told us they'd get back in touch with us on Monday and ask us to come back if necessary. We walked out feeling good, but also feeling very anxious.

"Venture capitalists have much more money than angel investors, so there's more at stake and they have different priorities. They want to take companies public and make *big* money and they're only going to invest if they are convinced the company has a real shot of making it big. That weekend of waiting is when I first started to understand how complicated life as a business-owner could be—my life is about making money for other people. Sure, if things go well I get money too and I can spend it on whatever I want. But I don't have a dime if some very rich people don't decide to give me some of their money so they can make more. Don't get me wrong, it wasn't all dark and depressing—it was just a new reality. I'm pondering and processing all this heavy stuff about how my fate is in the hands of wealthy strangers, but while I'm doing it I'm sitting at Yankee Stadium talking to Alex about getting rich. Over the weekend we went to two Yankees games, saw Paul Simon at Madison Square Garden, took a boat cruise around Manhattan, did a bus tour, ate fantastic food—tourist stuff. The whole time we were talking about how to spend money we hoped we'd have. It was exciting.

"But Monday morning things changed. We sat around the hotel in shorts and T-shirts with our day-two suits on hangers and waited for the phone to ring. We were in the middle of room-service burgers when it rang. Thirty minutes later we were back in the same office we'd left on Friday. They told us they were prepared to offer us $15 million for 30% of the company. I'd decided beforehand that we shouldn't let them have more than 25%, no matter how much they offered. We negotiated. They gave us $15 million for 25% of the company. That was it. I thought it was a great deal. They must have, too. We shook hands with all of them and walked out and down the hall to the elevator. It was just the two of us in the elevator and the doors closed. I punched the button for the ground floor and looked at the reflection of my shocked face in the stainless steel. Alex stood next to me looking at his reflection and said quietly, as if we were being watched, 'Fifteen million. Bensen, tell me we get some of that.' I didn't say anything until we were on the ground floor. For one, it was hard to talk, but I also didn't want Alex to react and wreck the elevator. We walked out of the elevator and I said, 'Some. We get some.' Alex shouted 'Yes!' and celebrated like he'd just beat the buzzer from half-court to win an NCAA championship. Everyone in the lobby looked our way. Alex didn't notice. He gave several fist pumps and slapped me on the back—hard—and walked all the way to the door with both fists high in the air. He knew 'some' meant way more than either of us had ever seen."

"How much?"

"Well, it was the same deal as before with angel investors—we had to use all of that money on the business. But, because of the amount of money and the amount of income that would be generated as we grew through the Chick-fil-A deal, we could pay ourselves decent salaries, get our own homes, upgrade vehicles—that kind of thing."

"So did you have to calm Alex down?"

"No," Mr. Bensen said.

"Really? But it's like he was thinking he was gonna go yacht shopping or something."

"No. Alex's family never had much when he was growing up. He still owed money on student loans. He had different priorities than I did, but the bottom line of what he wanted to do was get his own place and raise the standard of living for his parents. He was thrilled to be able to do that. We'd talked over that weekend about lots of things we'd like to do—but that's what he said he'd do first, and that's what he did.

"Still, we did celebrate. We sepnt way too much on dinner that night—still the best steak I've ever had—and we planned. It was just as exciting, but much more practical than the dreaming we'd done over the weekend. We talked about reasonable salaries, reasonably priced housing, reasonably priced cars for ourselves, and of course that led us to discussing all the ways we'd need to expand Caspian Sea. We were due to fly out in two days, but I called and got us switched to an afternoon flight the next day—we'd had fun in New York but there was way too much we needed to do to justify being gone another day. The afternoon flight allowed us time to visit Wall Street the following morning for the ringing of the bell at the New York Stock Exchange. You ever watch that?"

"Nope."

"9.30. Every morning. Watch it at least once. Every morning it's some VIP ringing the bell to signal the beginning of the trading day. This particular day it was a guy whose company just went public. I'd first seen it watching *Wall Street*—never really set it up as any kind of dream to aspire to or anything, but knew it was a big deal. But when we were there, I realized that's where I wanted to be—ringing that bell. The crazy thing about it was that, after the weekend we'd just had, it was actually a reasonable goal. I'd explained the significance of all of it to Alex on the way downtown so, by the time we got there we both understood it as something exciting but also intimidating—something that represented lots of work left to be done. It was some guy in his fifties from Wisconsin with the bell. Alex and I stood and watched—enraptured—and swallowed big when he rang it. We took a cab to JFK. When we got to the airport I went to the desk at the gate and asked if there was room for Alex and me in first class. The lady said there was only room for one of us and she added, 'Of course, I'll have to charge you for that.' 'Of course,' I replied. Alex denies it, but I promise I saw a tear in his eye when we stepped on the plane and the flight attendant showed him his seat."

"That's huge—that weekend in New York—that's like a movie right there," Derek said.

He no longer had to try to think like a student instead of a spy. Criminal or not, Mr. Bensen told an inspiring story and Derek was wondering if he'd be able to handle those situations Mr. Bensen seemed to handle so well.

"No, there's not enough struggle to make it a good story—and there's no conclusion, no end—it's just a couple of excited kids looking around at big buildings. Maybe if you throw in the Hollywood ending of me ringing the bell on Wall Street ... "

"You did it? You rang that bell?"

Mr. Bensen got up, walked over to a shelf, picked up a framed photo, and brought it back to Derek.

"Hah. That's you—a little more hair. No Alex?"

"Yup. Alex didn't make the trip. It's probably silly to keep that photo out, but that was a huge day."

"So you were on TV and all?"

"Yeah, but that's not why it was huge. We were public. We became huge."

"I still don't know what that means," Derek said.

"Okay. So we left New York and went back home with $15 million as well as five new owners. We already had the angel investors in addition to Alex, Spencer, and me. That was two years after Natasha and the angel investors—four years total since the week at the lake when Caspian Sea was born. You know how you feel like four years is a career when you're in high school or when you're in college? It's not so much about the time frame, but that period in your development is so unique and important. That's kind of how our first four years was—like high school. Then the college four years started when we went to New York."

"Sorry, but what's that have to do with going public? I still don't really know what that means," Derek interrupted.

"Okay, but slow down, huh? I just made a nice little analogy for you. Going public. When anyone says *go public* they mean *become a publicly traded company*. Coca-Cola is a publicly traded company, Chick-fil-A is a private company. Both are impressive companies with great management. I own shares of Coke. You can own some, too. Shares of Coke are traded on the New York Stock Exchange. Anyone with a brokerage account and enough money can buy as many shares as he or she wants. I would love to own a piece of Chick-fil-A. I can't. They aren't traded anywhere. They (the current owners of Chick-fil-A) decide who can or cannot buy shares. It's invitation only. It's just like when Alex and I started Caspian Sea. We were the owners. Alex owned 50% and I owned 50%. If Alex wanted to, he could sell part of his 50% to you but I would have to approve it.

"Publicly traded companies are required to release financial data and other information that privately held companies aren't. If you want to know how much cash Coke has on its *Balance Sheet* you can find out on any number of websites. One quick search and you've got it. If you want to know the same information for Chick-fil-A, you're out of luck. You can ask nicely, but they don't have to tell. Make sense?"

"I think so."

"Here's the biggest difference. What's the goal of financial management?"

"To maximize shareholder wealth," Derek answered.

"Correct—for publicly traded companies. For private companies the goal is whatever the company wants it to be. Imagine that Chick-fil-A management did something stupid like changing the recipe for their chicken or replacing the cookies and cream milkshake with a fat-free pomegranate smoothie."

"Terrible," Derek said. "I'm there three days a week, mostly for that milkshake. No way pomegranates, or whatever, are going to maximize shareholder wealth."

"But they don't have to maximize shareholder wealth. Maybe they want to promote pomegranate consumption? They're free to engage in whatever money-destroying, consumer-alienating activities they want. There's nothing you or I can do to stop them. It's their company. It's literally none of our business. On the other hand, Coke is different. If the management of Coke did something ridiculous like only sell Coke out of vending machines every other Tuesday from noon until 6:00 pm, then what should I, a shareholder, do?"

"Sell your stock. Obviously that's a bad decision and Coke is about to lose a lot of money," Derek answered.

"Right. And other investors will sell their Coke stock. No one will want to buy and the price will crash. Then some smart guys get together and realize that Coke is still a great company. It's just that the current management made a dumb decision. They buy up a bunch of shares for virtually nothing. Shareholders get to vote for the board of directors. The board hires and fires management. In this case, fires. These smart guys buy enough shares to be able to put their people on the board. Those people then fire the current CEO and his people. They then hire new managers who run the company right. Of course, that would never happen, but you get the point, right?"

"Yeah," Derek said. "I think so. A private company like Chick-fil-A can run their business any way they want to. A public company like Coke has to maximize shareholder wealth. If investors don't like the way management is running the company, then they can sell their stock or they can elect a new board who'll hire better management. So what's the advantage of going public? You have to release financial statements, jump through all these hoops, and if you make your shareholders mad, they can fire you. Why not stay private?" Derek asked.

"Money. There are other reasons, but to be perfectly honest, money was our primary reason. Remember how Caspian Sea started? It was a great idea but we needed money to buy the equipment and supplies we needed in order to grow. We could borrow some of what we needed but not all of it. Spencer was the first new owner, then the angel investors, then the venture capitalists. Each round of financing was more money for Caspian Sea to use to grow. We were successful and I was a millionaire on paper."

"What do you mean on paper?"

"I owned 18.375% of a company that was worth—well I don't even know what it was worth. I don't know what it was worth because I couldn't sell it. I couldn't call up my broker and sell 10,000 shares for $20 per share. We were private. Once we became public, I could sell. Anybody who wanted to could buy. Now the owners of the company weren't a handful of guys who were financial experts and who could all fit in a conference room. Mutual funds, pension funds, day-traders, individual investors, anybody, thousands of people were part owners. I worked for them now. You getting it?"

"Yeah, I think. You said it was five years between the New York trip and you going public?"

"Yeah. Good years—really good years—but tough years."

"How so?"

"It was all of that pressure I mentioned before about working to make money for other people. I'm not asking for sympathy, but it does come with a great deal of responsibility that is difficult to handle. Some people see me and they really love Caspian Sea and they kind of picture me sitting around smiling about all the kids and parents and happy people enjoying a refreshing drink all across the country. I stopped thinking about that somewhere in those first two years. Alex developed the product and we made it available to the public—that was all done in a few months. Since then, it's all been maintaining it—not so people can keep drinking it, but so the investors can keep making money. I'm happy that people enjoy the drink along the way, and I hope my employees benefit from working for the company, but my priority always has to be the pockets of the shareholders. If the shareholders are unhappy, they sell their shares, or they fire me. Feeling the weight of all of that and managing that weight with judgment calls and tough decisions is what made those years tough."

"What made them good?"

"I started living. We started living. Alex and I started benefiting from the work and seeing how we—and others—could continue to benefit more. After New York, I did some research and Alex and I settled on modest but adequate salaries for ourselves. We kept the original building, but bought office space nearby and hired people to oversee various aspects of daily operations. We opened up a few more production plants, bought trucks for distribution, and launched a marketing program. It was work. The priority was to make sure Caspian Sea kept making money, to keep the investors happy and convince them that we could go public and grow. We did a good job of it, but we also had fun. I met my wife a few months after we got back from New York. We were married a couple years later—started having kids."

"Alex? Did he get married?"

"Nope. Never has. He was engaged—once. But he's happy—always has been. His 'happy' is just different from mine. When we each bought our own homes it became apparent how different we were. For the most part it was a healthy difference—we sort of balanced each other out. I was practical and becoming more practical—he had always been a little more impulsive and spontaneous and he was becoming more so. There were times in the business that we needed to be more of one than the other and we usually made it work. However—" Mr. Bensen stopped himself. "Wait. We're getting hung up here a little. Where are we in the story?"

"Wait, what do you mean *however*? What happened with Alex?"

"I'll get to that—it's not a big deal, really. Where were we in the story?"

"After New York, you came back and worked and expanded and grew and got married."

"Yeah, so that was, like I said, like the college stage—like five years of college. Four years of high school preceded that, and we graduated from that four years when we got the 15 million. I guess you could say graduation from the five-year stage was the bell-ringing, but it's more complicated than that. It was a little over five years after the New York trip when we actually hit the billion dollar sales mark."

"Hold on, a billion?"

"Yeah, but—"

"But nothing, that's a billion dollars, that's huge!"

"Yeah, but it's just a mark, really."

Derek was shaking his head.

"Seriously," Mr. Bensen continued. "You can't think about money as anything but a measuring tool unless you're making a deposit into your own personal account. I'm not diminishing the fact that I was making good money and living comfortably—I'm just saying that a billion dollars in sales doesn't translate into filthy rich—it's a measuring stick—a milestone.

"The significance of reaching that milestone is we knew we were ready to go public—and so did all the investors. But you don't just go public. You do another round of meetings and presentations known as a *road show*—meetings in different cities with big-time money managers—people who are paid to make decisions with other people's millions. This is that one example when Alex and I had trouble reconciling differences."

"The one you started telling before?"

"Yeah. So Alex heard the term *road show* and he was all excited. He saw us driving all over the country, in and out of a new city every day—eating great food, staying in great hotels, having a ball. But, your average road show hits only three cities: New York, Boston, and San Francisco—sometimes Chicago. Alex didn't like the sound of that, and it was all because he'd gotten this sort of traveling carnival thing in his head. Long story short, our road show was Boston, New York, Chicago, Dallas, Los Angeles, San Francisco—three unnecessary stops. Alex drove the whole way—in his Ferrari."

"Nice. What color?"

"Red."

"Nice."

"The rest of us flew."

"The rest of who?"

"Our team. No more Alex and me walking into offices with *Balance Sheets* and/or T-shirts. I knew every detail about the situation of the company from every angle, but we paid people to process that information and figure out how to present it. We were only really there to show that we were personally invested in it. I talked in the meetings, but anything I said was just to support what the team had presented. It was easy. That part anyway. What wasn't easy was keeping up with Alex—or him keeping up with us. No kidding, there was one person on the team specifically tasked with praying that Alex got to the next town safely."

"Did he drink?"

"It wasn't that—we were on a schedule. He was driving a Ferrari cross-country, sometimes twelve hours straight. Any complication—accident, flat tire, empty gas tank—could jeopardize our road show. The meetings were easy, as long as we were all there."

"Did he make them all?"

"Every one—but in Dallas and L.A. we had no idea where he was until five minutes before the meeting. You're laughing, but it was unacceptable. Seriously. I spent many hours trying to figure out the consequences of firing him."

"Really?"

"Don't give me that *really*? You like him because he's the cool guy with the cool car—the rebel. But you can't be that guy when you're responsible for all we were responsible for. Especially not publicly. We were going public—that was the point of those road show meetings—to announce to potential investors that we were going public and convince them we were worth buying into—so we could grow as big as possible as quickly as possible. But the other side of going public is we became immediately subjected to a whole new set of rules and regulations. Financial statements, income statements, cash flow charts—all of that stuff we used to produce for our own benefit and use as we saw fit—all of it becomes public information."

"Public. Makes sense."

"Yeah. So, not that Alex ever did anything I'm aware of that needed to be covered up, but he didn't operate in such a way that kept accountability as simple as possible. Accountability—compliance—is always going to be complicated. I saw some of Alex's patterns making things potentially way too complicated."

Derek hadn't written a note in quite a while. He wrote down: *Alex. Road trip. Dallas/L.A. cover-up???* Then he asked, "So, did you fire him?"

"I didn't have to. In addition to Alex actually making all the meetings, they were a success. The point of a road show is to get as many potential investors as possible to verbally commit to buying as many shares of stock as possible—they call this *book building.* This is when Spencer's mom finally started to reap some benefit from being so kind to us so many times. She's an investment banker. Investment bankers buy stock from a company, like Caspian Sea, and then sell the stock to investors. So she was in touch with most of the folks we met with on the road show, and she was in touch with us—with me. She needed to buy from us at a reasonable price, and then sell to other investors at a reasonable price."

"Who says what's *reasonable* in that situation?"

"Exactly. She wants to make money, but she also needs to keep the business owners happy and the investors happy so they're willing to continue to do business with her. The relationship between investment bankers and business owners and investors is very complicated."

"So why didn't you have to fire Alex?"

"About a month after the road show, that picture was taken." Mr. Bensen pointed to the New York Stock Exchange photo. "We were public. Alex knew he wasn't cut out for a career of making money for others and waiting patiently for anything. About six months after we went public, he sold most of his stock and retired."

"How much did he make?"

"Honestly, I don't even know that. I do know he's doing just fine, and so is his family. He's got an accountant we both trust and he's healthy and smiling and genuinely happy every time I see him. You'd be happy to know he still drives the Ferrari too."

"Did it change much not having him around?"

"Not really. I'd been handling most of the business decisions with our executive staff anyway. I moved someone else into his official R & D role and we kept on going."

"Making money."

"Yup. Making money. But I also started the Liquidity Foundation and looked for ways the success of Caspian Sea could benefit people who have real deep needs. It's still a lot of work and I'm still making money for other people, but I think I've found a healthy balance between work and life—between profit and benefit.

"We went public seven years ago. About two months ago we reached the $3 billion sales mark. Don't go wild."

"Measuring stick—I've got it," Derek said. Then added under his breath, but so Mr. Bensen could hear, "made out of solid gold, a mile long and a city block thick."

"Ha. Here's a couple more measuring sticks. Promise to keep your seat?"

Derek nodded.

"The market value of Caspian Sea was $8.5 billion. Coke had been interested in us for a while, but when we hit that mark we settled and they bought Caspian Sea for $10 billion. We're now a wholly owned subsidiary of Coke, but I'm still CEO. And here we are, sitting in my office."

"Wow. That's the story?"

"That's it."

VIII

Toth (as Moss) walked up and stood next to Derek at the same spot Stovall had met him a week before. "See, no worries," Moss said.

Derek flinched a bit and looked up at him.

"Don't look at me. Wait until we get to the park." They walked along into the same park, and sat on the same bench. "See. No Stovall, none of this Toth character—just you and me. How'd it go with Bensen?"

"I don't know. I took notes. Got some names."

"Yeah, gimme that. Lemme see those." Moss looked over the sheet and feigned interest, then tore it out of the notebook and folded it and put it in his inside jacket pocket. "Any formula talk?"

"Believe it or not, there was—unintentionally, sort of," Derek said. He could tell Moss was interested. "It was nothing really. I asked him what the secret was to a successful business and he thought I was asking about what was in the drink and he said, 'ice.'" Derek waited for Moss to acknowledge the joke. He didn't. "There was ice in the glasses—we were drinking Caspian Sea there in his office and there was ice in it."

"So what? What about the formula?"

"Then, later on, he told me about how the guy made the first batch of it at some lake house and he used oranges and lemons and plums—that's about all I got."

"Oranges, lemons, and plums."

"Yeah."

"You're gonna have to do better than that, son."

"What happens if I don't get it?"

"You giving up on me already? Why?"

"No. I'm just—" Derek leaned back on the bench and looked at the trees. "I mean, there were a few things he said that lined up with what you said about him trying to look like Mr. Nice Guy."

"Told ya."

"Yeah, but they could line up with him actually being a genuinely good person."

Moss stared at Derek for several seconds before responding. "Why is he seeing you once a week? Because he's a good person? He can be a good person by buying everyone in Africa a new laptop or something. Why does he have you in his office once a week? It doesn't make sense unless there's something in it for him."

Derek sat and thought for a few seconds. "Okay. I still don't really get it. And I don't see how I'm gonna get the formula out of him. Why would he tell me anything like that?"

"I'm working on that part. You just keep meeting him and being a student. You're all set up with Stovall Enterprises? You're on the payroll?"

"Yeah, as far as I know."

"Good. You let me know if Stovall doesn't make good on his offer."

Derek said nothing.

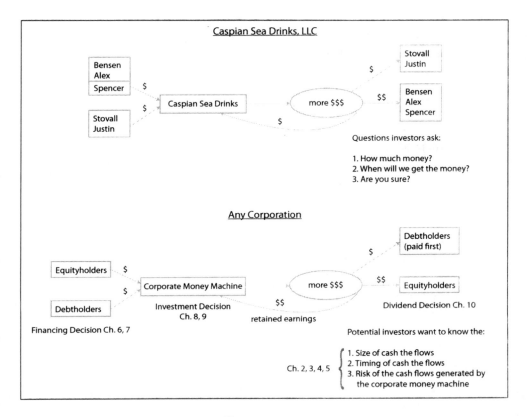

Caspian Sea Drinks, LLC

Questions investors ask:

1. How much money?
2. When will we get the money?
3. Are you sure?

Any Corporation

Financing Decision Ch. 6, 7

Investment Decision Ch. 8, 9

retained earnings

Dividend Decision Ch. 10

Potential investors want to know the:

Ch. 2, 3, 4, 5

1. Size of cash the flows
2. Timing of cash the flows
3. Risk of the cash flows generated by the corporate money machine

QUESTIONS

1. What does Mr. Bensen say the goal of financial management should be? Do you agree?
2. If the goal of the firm is to maximize shareholder wealth, should Mr. Bensen donate Caspian Sea Drinks' money or just his own money to the Liquidity Foundation?
3. Does Mr. Bensen's involvement with charitable causes make you more or less likely to buy stock in Caspian Sea Drinks?
4. Mr. Bensen wants to mentor someone who has character. What does he mean when he tells Derek that it matters "who you are"? Are ethics important? Explain.

5. Spencer bought shares in Caspian Sea Drinks while Stovall loaned money to Caspian Sea Drinks. Both transactions occurred at the same time when the company was young. Did Spencer or Stovall take the greater risk?

6. From a purely financial standpoint, and without regard to ethics, could it have made sense for Eric, Alex, and Spencer to gamble their $33,000 in an attempt to make a $119,000 loan payment and avoid bankruptcy? Do shareholders and bondholders always agree on what actions management should take? Why or why not?

7. After angel investors bought a piece of Caspian Sea Drinks did the incentives of Eric and Alex change?

8. How is a private company different from a publicly traded one?

9. Why are publicly traded companies required to release large amounts of financial data?

10. What do you think are the advantages and disadvantages of a sole proprietorship, partnership, LLC, and publicly-traded corporation?

11. Derek randomly found Stovall when he needed financing to keep Caspian Sea Drinks in business. Why do you think markets are important?

12. Stovall appears to be a relatively wealthy person. How could he feel poor?

13. Is Finance all about making money for yourself or do Finance professionals have any obligation to help others?

14. Did any of the characters in the story have a job that appealed to you? If so, which one?

15. Are you willing to put in the practice to learn the fundamentals of Corporate Finance?

CHAPTER 2

TIME VALUE OF MONEY I:
THE MECHANICS OF SIMPLE MAGIC MONEY
MACHINES

H ello Derek," a cheery Mrs. Howe said. "He said to wait inside. He'll be back any minute."

"Thank you." Mr. Bensen's office door was closed. Derek opened it, walked in, put his notebook down on the now familiar table and sat down. The door clicked closed. Derek wondered if there were surveillance cameras in the room. *There had to be.* He looked around the corners of the room. *But why would he have to have cameras? It's not like he'd keep a ton of money or the secret formula in a safe in his office. Would he?*

The door opened. "Hey! What are you doing in here?"

Derek gulped and sat up, "She—Mrs. Howe said—"

"Relax. Get up," Mr. Bensen said, "We're going to another room."

Derek picked up his notebook and followed Mr. Bensen down the hall. He wondered if maybe they were fitting the office with cameras since they knew he was going to be coming more regularly. Walking down the hall he tried to figure out a way to say, "This is a very nice office," without sounding like his mom.

Without turning around, Mr. Bensen said, "This is the house Caspian Sea built."

"Nice house," Derek said, and felt good about it.

"Funny though, how little we actually talk about soft drinks." Mr. Bensen stopped outside a room and motioned Derek inside.

"We'll spend hours in these rooms and never say the words *refreshing* or *delicious*." They walked into a basic conference room with a large polished wooden table surrounded by soft leather chairs on wheels. The curtains were pulled back to reveal views of the windows of surrounding buildings.

"Sit anywhere," Mr. Bensen said. "Tell me what you think Finance is. Define it."

Derek sat at the end of the table closest to the whiteboard on the wall, facing the wall of windows. "Finance is the science of managing money," he said. Mr. Bensen walked around the table and sat across from Derek.

"Okay, fine. I went to class too. But don't you find that definition limiting? Is that why you're a Finance major? Because you hope to become a professional money scientist? Finance is the study of money machines—magic money machines."

"Okay," Derek said.

"Here, I'll teach you the core concept of Finance. See that printer over there in the corner? That's not a printer. That's a money machine. Exactly one year from today it will print $10,000. I want to sell it. How much will you give me for it right now?"

"I don't know. Do I just pick a number?"

"You answer the question. Don't overthink it. You have no doubt that money machine will do what I say it will do. The question really is how much would you give up today to get $10,000 in one year?

"$9,130?" Derek said, half asking.

"Sold! Now, what if I told you the money machine would pay $10,000 exactly two years from today instead of one? Would you pay me more or less than $9,130 for it?"

"Less."

"Good. One more question. What if I told you the money machine would flip a coin. Heads it pays you $20,000 in one year, tails it pays you nothing. Would you pay me more or less than $9,130 for it?"

"Less."

"Smart. See. That's Finance."

"I don't get it."

"Finance is about buying and selling money machines. Every money machine has its own payout rule. All you need to know is the rule. The rule tells you the size, timing, and risk of the cash flows that the money machine promises to produce. Size—the bigger, the better. Timing—the sooner, the better. Risk—the less, the better."

"Okay. I guess the hard part is coming up with an exact number."

"Right. The next step is coming up with exact numbers. We need some math so we can find precise answers. The math isn't hard. You just gotta make sure you remember how to use a calculator and you might need to dust off your Algebra. The important thing is to know why you are doing each calculation. Remember: size, timing, risk. Here are some Caspian Sea examples.

"You remember me talking about Stovall?"

"Stovall, yeah, sure." Derek hadn't thought about Stovall for a few minutes and didn't like being reminded of him.

"Stovall bought a money machine from Caspian Sea. It was called a bond. The rule was simple—Caspian Sea will pay $108,000 in exactly one year. Stovall paid $100,000 for it.

"You remember Spencer? He bought another money machine from Caspian Sea—a stock. The rule was more complicated. It promised to pay ... well, it's complicated. Spencer paid $40,000 to get 30% of whatever money was left over after Caspian Sea paid what it owed to everyone else. So he didn't know the size of the cash flows. And Caspian Sea might not pay money ... we'll get to that later. Just know that some money machines, like stock, can be complex. We'll cover them after you really understand the simple ones.

"When Caspian Sea buys equipment to make more of the delicious and refreshing drink we hardly ever talk about in here, it's buying a money machine. After all, we're in the business to make money, not refreshing and delicious drinks. That equipment will produce Caspian Sea which will produce money. We estimate the size, timing, and risk of the cash flows the machine will produce before we decide how much we're willing to pay for it.

"To start with I'll give you the rule. I'll tell you the size, timing, and risk of a money machine. You'll tell me what it's worth. We'll start with simple rules, then move on to complex ones. Then we'll talk about how to estimate the size, timing, and risk for different kinds of money machines. We'll focus on three types of money machines—bonds, stocks, and projects. Along the way you'll see why each one is important. You have to really, truly understand the concepts and master the calculations.

"Let's start over here with our printer, the money machine. It will pay exactly $10,000 in one year. You said you'd pay me $9,130 for it. Why?"

"To make money."

"Okay. But be precise with your language. You don't want money. You want what money will buy. You are willing to give up what $9,130 will buy today so you can have what $10,000 will buy in exactly one year. We need to translate that to the language of math." Mr. Bensen stood and walked up to the board and picked up a marker. "Here's the formula. Ha," he paused. "I feel like a teacher.

$$10,000 = 9,130 * (1 + r)^1$$

"That formula tells me that the amount the money machine will produce in the future, $10,000, is equal to the amount you would pay for it today, $9,130, times $(1 + r)^1$. That r is key. It's the interest rate. If you tell me your interest rate then I can figure out what you would be willing to pay for any money machine. In this case it is 0.09529 or 9.529%. Rearrange the formula like this.

$$9,130 = \frac{10,000}{1.09529^1}$$

"Again. What are the three things you need to know about a money machine?" Mr. Bensen asked.

"Size, timing, and risk."

"Let's start with size. What would you pay for a money machine that pays $20,000 in one year?"

Derek looked out the window to do some math. "$18,260? If I'd pay $9,130 to get $10,000 in one year then I'd pay twice that to receive twice that."

"Good insight. Now do the math to prove you're right." Mr. Bensen pointed to the board.

Derek stood up and wrote:

$$X = \frac{20,000}{1.09529^1} = 18,260.00$$

"Okay. Stay there. Now let's talk timing. What if the $10,000 came in two years, not in one year?"

Derek wrote:

$$X = \frac{10,000}{1.09529^2} = 8,335.69$$

"Is that right?" he asked.

"Yup. Now let's write down the formula." Mr. Bensen picked up another marker and wrote:

$$V_0 = \frac{V_n}{(1+r)^n}$$

"V_0 is the value of the money machine today. V_n is the amount of money the money machine will pay you n years from today."

"Okay. So risk is next?"

"Not yet. We'll get to risk in a few weeks. Let's look at the same problem, but from a few different angles. Assume you have $10,000 to invest and your interest rate is 10%. How much must a money machine pay you in one year for you to be willing to buy it?"

Derek thought for a minute then said, "All I have to do is rearrange the equation. Now:

$$V_n = V_0(1 + r)^n$$

So $V_n = 10{,}000 * 1.10^1 = 11{,}000$.

"There you go. Two more things for this week. One, I'm going to give you a lot of problems to make sure you can use the formula. But first, I want to make sure you understand what the interest rate really means. It allows me to figure out how much you're willing to pay today to get a certain amount of money in the future. When you pay money today you're willingly giving up the ability to buy stuff now. You'll only do this because you'll be able to buy more stuff in the future. For example, you said you'd give up $9,130 today to get $10,000 in one year. Does that mean you can buy $870 worth of more stuff in one year?"

Derek thought but didn't respond.

"The answer is no," Mr. Bensen continued. "Suppose the wife and I are thinking about taking a vacation. The total cost of the trip is $9,130. We could buy that money machine and have $10,000 for a vacation next year. We'd be willing to do that if we could upgrade to better rooms, stay another day or do something with the extra money that would be fun. But prices go up. If we book the exact same trip next year it will cost more. So to get us to give up the $9,130 today, we have to be compensated for the increase in the price of the trip and get enough additional money to be able to do something fun enough to make us willing to wait. In Finance talk we need a *real rate of return* (being able to upgrade the trip) plus an *inflation premium* (getting enough money to cover the price increase).

"That make sense?"

"Yeah. Barely. I get it, but I'm not sure I could explain it."

"It'll make more sense as you use it in problems. Listen," Mr. Bensen checked his watch. "Our time is about up. At the end of each of these meetings I'm going to give you one of these." He held up a manila envelope. "It's a Study Packet that has all the equations and definitions you need plus a problem set. Here you go."

Derek wasn't thrilled with getting what looked like extra homework, but he didn't complain. "Okay. Thanks. This has gotta be extra work for you."

"A little, but believe it or not it's fun. Shocking." They both stood and shook hands. "Next week," Mr. Bensen said. "Come back and ask me questions about anything."

"I will," said Derek.

STUDY PACKET: TIME VALUE OF MONEY I

Definitions

Discounting—calculating the present value of a set of cash flows.

Discount Rate—the interest rate used in time value of money calculations.

Future Value—the value of a set of cash flows after their occurrence. The context of the question will indicate the exact future time for which future value is to be calculated.

Present Value—the value of a set of cash flows prior to their occurrence. The term *present* should not be taken literally. It does not necessarily mean today. The context of the question will indicate the exact timing for which present value is to be calculated.

Equations

Time Value of Money

Start with the equation that is perhaps the most important one in all of Finance:

(2.1)
$$FV = PV(1 + r)^t$$

where FV is future value, PV is present value, r is the interest rate, and t is the amount of time between PV and FV. An alternative way to express the same relationship is:

(2.2)
$$V_n = V_0(1 + i)^n$$

where V_n is the value of the cash flow at time n and V_0 is the value of the cash flow today (at time zero). The symbols i and n are the same as r and t in the first equation. Different people tend to use different variable names to express the same relationship.

Finally, to the most mathematically pure way to express the relationship:

(2.3)
$$V_{n+k} = V_n(1 + i)^k$$

This equation is more general. It describes the relationship of a cash flow at any time, n, to the cash flow at any other time, n+k.

Nominal, Real, and Inflation Rates

(2.4)
$$(1 + R) = (1 + r)(1 + h)$$

$$R = r + h + rh$$

$$(2.5) \qquad\qquad R \approx r + h$$

where R is the nominal interest rate, r is the real interest rate, and h is the rate of inflation. The nominal interest rate is the named or stated interest rate. The real interest rate reflects the anticipated increase in purchasing power. The inflation rate is the increase in the cost of a basket of goods and services.

Typically, inflation is measured by CPI. Regardless of how inflation is measured, it is not a precise number. A full description of the difficulties of measuring inflation is beyond the scope of this book. For our purposes, the following thought experiment is sufficient. Imagine going into a store where everything is sold. You fill your basket and pay $100 for the contents. You return next year and buy the same items but the cost is $110. Inflation, therefore, was 10%. This methodology works great for items that do not change like bread and milk. However, it does not work as well for items like computers that continually improve due to technological advancement. Nor does it work for newly created goods and services. A thorough investigation into the art and science of measuring inflation is fascinating. For now, just remember that it is a soft number.

Rather than using the precise relationship given in equation 2.4, many Finance professionals use the approximate relationship given in equation 2.5. From a practical standpoint the approximation is sufficient.

PROBLEM SET

Finding Present Value

1. Solve equation 2.1 for PV.
2. An investor will be willing to pay $\_\_\_\_\_$ today for a money machine that will produce $2,000 three years from today. Assume the appropriate interest rate is 10%.
3. An investor will be indifferent between receiving $\_\_\_\_\_$ today or $6,000 five years from today. Assume the appropriate interest rate is 7%.
4. Suppose an investor will need to have $50,000 in an account in 13 years and that the account pays 5%. She must deposit $\_\_\_\_\_$ in the account today.
5. If you raise the interest rate in problems 2–4, will the solutions be higher or lower? What if you lower the interest rate?

Finding Future Value

6. Suppose you deposit $1,000 into an account today that earns 10%. In three years the account will be worth $\_\_\_\_\_$.
7. Suppose you deposit $3,000 into an account today that earns 10%. In three years the account will be worth $\_\_\_\_\_$.
8. Suppose you deposit $3,000 into an account today that earns 10%. In five years the account will be worth $\_\_\_\_\_$.
9. Notice that a larger deposit results in a higher future value. Notice that leaving the deposit in the account results in a higher future value. Although this is a somewhat simple observation, it is important. To the extent possible make sure the answer to each problem you solve makes sense. Doing so will sharpen your intuition and minimize careless errors. This principle holds for

CHAPTER 2

every problem in this book as well as in real world problems where your answers may make or lose real money. In this case we know that size and timing matter. Repeat 6–8 with an interest rate of 11%. Then repeat with an interest rate of 9%. Do your answers make sense?

Finding the Interest Rate

10. Solve 2.1 for r.
11. Suppose an investor is willing to pay no more than $1,000 for a money machine that will produce $1,200 three years from today. The investor used a discount rate of ____% to value the machine.
12. Suppose you deposit $2,000 into an account today. In five years the account is worth $3,000. The account earned ____%.
13. Suppose an investor is indifferent between receiving $10,000 today and $20,000 13 years from today. The investor is using a discount rate of ____%.

Finding Time

14. Solve 2.1 for t.
15. Suppose you deposit $1,000 into an account today that earns 10%. It will take ____ years for the account to be worth $1,600.
16. Suppose you deposit $3,000 into an account today that earns 7%. It will take ____ years for the account to be worth $4,900.
17. Suppose you deposit $25,000 into an account today that earns 5%. It will take ____ years for the account to be worth $50,000.

Nominal, Real, and Inflation Rates

18. Assume the real rate of return is 3% and the inflation rate is 2%. Find the nominal rate of return using the exact formula then using the approximation.
19. Assume the real rate of return is 5% and the inflation rate is 4%. Find the nominal rate of return using the exact formula then using the approximation.
20. Assume the nominal rate of return is 7% and the real rate of return is 3%. Find the inflation rate using the exact formula then using the approximation.
21. Assume the nominal rate of return is 8% and the inflation rate is 5%. Find the real rate of return using the exact formula then using the approximation.

In the previous problem set we assumed that deposits were made today. In the next set of problems deposits will be made at various times. Here it will be helpful to think in terms of equation 2.3.

22. Suppose you deposit $1,000 into an account five years from today that earns 10%. Eight years from today the account will be worth $_____.
23. Suppose you deposit $3,000 into an account seven years from today that earns 7%. Fifteen years from today the account will be worth $_____.
24. Suppose you deposit $25,000 into an account two years from today that earns 5%. Ten years from today the account will be worth $_____.
25. Suppose you need to have $2,000 in an account ten years from today and that the account pays 10%. You must have $_____ in the account two years from today.

26. Suppose you need to have $6,000 in an account fourteen years from today and that the account pays 7%. You must have $_____ in the account three years from today.

27. Suppose you need to have $50,000 in an account 20 years from today and that the account pays 5%. You must deposit $_____ in the account seven years from today.

28. Suppose you deposit $1,000 into an account four years from today. Twelve years from today the account is worth $1,400. The account earned ____%.

29. Suppose you deposit $1,000 into an account five years from today that earns 10%. It will be worth $1,600 _____ years from today.

30. Assume the real rate of interest is 3% and the inflation rate is 2%. What is the value today of receiving $10,000 in seven years?

2.1

Derek saw Moss through the glass doors before he walked out of the building. Moss stood by a trash can, smoking. When he saw Derek walk out, he flicked his cigarette into the trash can, raised his eyebrows at Derek and nodded toward the park. Derek walked in the direction of the park without looking again for Moss. When Derek reached the park he walked to the same bench and sat down with his notebook. Moss was right behind him.

"Okay kid," Moss said. "Talk to me. What've you got there?"

"Nothing really—I couldn't take any notes this time, there was too much going on. We were in a conference room with a whiteboard and everything. It was like class."

"And?"

"Nothing. We talked about money machines—size, timing, risk. Finance stuff," Derek said. "He uh ... he mentioned Stovall—"

"What? What'd he say?" asked Moss, eager for locker room leverage against Stovall.

"Nothing. I mean, just that Stovall bought a bond off him early on—a hundred thousand dollars."

"So what? We knew that. That's nothing," said Moss. "Anything about what's in the drink?"

"Nothing. I'm tellin' you, I don't know how I'm gonna get that. If I'm a student, I'm there to learn. He's all gung-ho teaching me stuff. Gave me homework and all." Derek held up the notebook. "I've gotta do this stuff or he's not gonna let me come back."

"So do it. Who's stopping you?"

"I'm just saying, I can't be in there, keeping up with all he's talking about, and also thinking about being a spy and trying to steer the conversation toward ingredients," Derek said.

Moss looked into the trees and didn't say anything.

"If you give me some questions to ask him or something to try to get him talking, I can try that. I've just got no instincts for being a spy."

"You're not a spy, kid. That's the problem. Spies are bad. You're a good kid. You're thinking about it all wrong. You're pursuing justice." Moss put his hand on Derek's shoulder. "You're one of the good guys. I'm one of the good guys. This is what good guys do—they help each other out. Bensen's bad. Trust me. I can't tell you how bad. Just know that you've got access to things that no one else can get to. If you get to those things, then you're a good guy who—guess what?—who becomes a hero." Moss looked at Derek like he expected Derek to cry an inspirational tear. Derek just looked bewildered. "That's the best kind of good guy there is, man. A hero!" Moss whispered passionately. "That can be you!" Moss patted Derek on the side of the neck with the palm of his hand, like an encouraging father. He'd seen it done in movies.

Derek didn't know what to say. He said, "Okay."

"Relax," said Moss. "Next week? Same time, same place?"

"Next week," Derek said.

Moss stood and walked out of the park.

—

The following week Derek arrived at Mr. Bensen's office carrying a three-ring binder with the completed problems from the week before in the same envelope. He rode up the elevator. He had no plan to try to get information for Moss. He knew Moss said Mr. Bensen was bad, but couldn't figure out how he could be. Even if he was bad and it was obvious, Derek wasn't the guy to get the information Moss wanted. Besides, Derek wasn't obliged to Moss in any way. He'd checked his bank balance every day since his meeting with Stovall's people and there were no deposits made. He was a student with a great opportunity to learn valuable things from an incredibly successful CEO. That was it. That was all it could be. He walked out of the elevator and into the office lobby where he was greeted by Mrs. Howe. "It must be Wednesday at 3:00," she said.

"Yes ma'am," Derek smiled.

"He said he'd meet you down the hall."

"Thanks," Derek said, happy that they weren't going to be back in Mr. Bensen's office. He was hopeful they'd never be back in his office. The more his meeting with Mr. Bensen felt like school, the less he felt like a spy. Moss's speech hadn't changed his feelings. Derek walked down to the conference room and sat where he'd sat the week before, looking out the windows at all the other windows facing him. "Money machines," he mumbled to himself.

"That's it," Mr. Bensen said as he walked into the room behind Derek and closed the door. Derek started to stand. Mr. Bensen put his hand on his shoulder and said, "Keep chillin'." He walked around and sat in his chair on the opposite side of the table. "So, any questions?"

"Mind if I have some of your tasty beverage?"

"Nice," Mr. Bensen grinned. "You've been waiting to squeeze that in, haven't you?"

"Not really, just keeping up with you."

"Great movie—massive cool points for that response. Now, any Finance questions?"

Derek couldn't think of another *Pulp Fiction* line he could fit in. "No, sir. I really don't have any. I feel pretty good about it all," Derek said. Mostly he felt good about his cool points.

CHAPTER 3

TIME VALUE OF MONEY II:
THE MECHANICS OF ADVANCED
MAGIC MONEY MACHINES

O k. We're going to talk about money machines a little more today but we'll soon get to some real practical stuff," Mr. Bensen said. "None of it is directly related to Caspian Sea. We'll get back to the Caspian Sea story—history—next week. *Time value of money* concepts apply to all areas of Finance, not just corporations. So, we'll work many types of problems. You've gotta take tons of ground balls in practice if you're gonna make plays in games.

"You can tell me the value of a money machine that makes one payment at some future time, or one that makes two payments, or even three. What about one that pays $1,000 per year for thirty years?"

Derek walked up to the board and picked up a marker. "Assuming my interest rate is 10% … " Derek began writing:

$$V_0 = \frac{1,000}{1.10^1} + \frac{1,000}{1.10^2} + \frac{1,000}{1.10^3} + \frac{1,000}{1.10^4} +$$

He stopped writing. "This is going to take a lot of time and board space. Do I have to do all thirty calculations and then add them up? There's gotta be a shorter way."

"Ha. There's never *gotta* be anything," Mr. Bensen said. "Think that way and you're set up for many disappointments. Ask if there *is* a way, but don't assume there's *gotta* be one. However, in this case, you're lucky. This is an *annuity*. Remember that word. An annuity is the same payment every period for a finite number of periods. This is a $1,000, 30-year annuity. The formula for the present value of an annuity is:

$$PVA_n = pmt * \frac{1 - \frac{1}{(1 + r)^n}}{r}$$

"The proof is there in the Study Packet," Mr. Bensen said and pointed to the envelope on the table under a calculator.

"So for this problem I have ... " Derek wrote on the board:

$$PVA_n = 1,000 * \frac{1 - \frac{1}{(1.10)^{30}}}{0.10} = 9,426.91$$

"That's shorter but it's still a nasty formula. It'd be pretty easy to make a mistake."

"Yeah. Check it out," Mr. Bensen said and picked up the calculator. "This knows the formula."

"Cool."

"Yeah. Notice precisely what the formula is for. It is the present value of an annuity that begins in exactly one year. These are more advanced problems so we need to draw timelines." Mr. Bensen went up to the board and wrote:

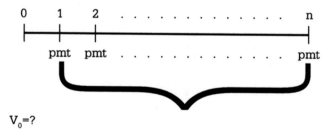

"Now, what if it was a 10-year, $500 annuity and the interest rate was 7%?" he asked Derek.

Derek wrote:

$$PVA_n = 500 * \frac{1 - \frac{1}{(1.07)^{10}}}{0.07} = 3,511.79$$

"What about a 27-year, $1,400 annuity at 5%?"
Derek wrote:

$$PVA_n = 1,400 * \frac{1 - \frac{1}{(1.05)^{27}}}{0.05} = 20,500.25$$

"By George, I think he's got it," Mr. Bensen chirped.

"What's that? *Mary Poppins?*" Derek asked.

"*My Fair Lady*, but pretty good guess. You've got it, huh?" Mr. Bensen pointed at the board. "Size, timing, and risk, right? Let's change the timing of the annuity. What if it started paying eight years from today? Here's where knowing what the formula means is important. Don't take the term *present value* literally. The formula tells you the value of the annuity one year before the payments start. That's the definition of *present value*—one period before the payments start."

Derek drew a new timeline on the board. "Okay. There's the value today of receiving $1,400 per year for 27 years with the first payment in exactly eight years.

$$V_7 = 1,400 * \frac{1 - \frac{1}{(1.05)^{27}}}{0.05} = 20,500.25$$

"The formula tells me the value in year 7 since it started paying in year 8. So I don't care if I get $20,500.25 in seven years or $1,400 per year for 27 years beginning in year 8. From last week I know that the value today of receiving $20,500.25 in seven years is:

$$V_0 = \frac{20,500.25}{1.05^7} = 14,569.14$$

"Okay. Good. Let's look at a different problem. What if you agreed to make payments of $1,000 per year for three years into an account that paid 10% interest? Draw the timeline." Derek drew it on the board. "This is still an annuity. The difference is we don't want to know the value today. We want to know the value exactly three years from today. You did this in the homework last week but didn't know it was an annuity." Mr. Bensen wrote the solution on the board.

$$V_3 = 1,000*1.10^2 + 1,000*1.10^1 + 1,000*1.10^0 = 3,310.00$$

Then he asked, "You want the good news or bad news first?"

"Bad news."

"The bad news is you'll have to find the future value of a 30-year annuity and that will take forever. The good news is there is a simple formula that is programmed into your calculator that will make this quick and easy. Here it is," Mr. Bensen said and wrote on the board:

$$FVA_n = pmt * \frac{(1+r)^n - 1}{r}$$

"So for this problem," he said and wrote:

$$FVA_3 = 1,000 * \frac{(1.10)^3 - 1}{0.10} = 3,310.00$$

"the important thing to remember," Mr. Bensen continued, "is that the formula gives you the value of the annuity on the day of the last payment and it assumes the payments start in one year. The present value annuity formula gave you the value of the annuity one year before the payments start. Remember that.

"I wanna see you do it. Suppose you make payments of $1,400 per year for 27 years into an account that pays 5%. What is the value of the annuity exactly 27 years from today?"

Derek drew a timeline and wrote:

$$FVA_{27} = 1,400 * \frac{(1.05)^{27} - 1}{0.05} = 76,536.78$$

"Nice. Now you can find the future value of a lump sum, the future value of an annuity, the present value of a lump sum, and the present value of an annuity. I'm gonna leave you here. You've got some paper right? Work on these problems. Then we'll add some twists and practical applications. I'll be back in a few minutes."

The door closed behind Mr. Bensen. Derek sat down and slumped in his chair. He was getting the material and he couldn't believe it was being presented to him by the CEO of a billion-dollar company. He thought for a second about Moss's suggestion that Mr. Bensen had an ulterior motive for inviting him to the office once a week. He daydreamed, staring out of the window for a minute, but then regained focus. He didn't know what *a few minutes* meant to Mr. Bensen and he didn't want to look lazy or slow.

About twenty minutes later, just as Derek was yawning and stretching after finishing the last problem, Mr. Bensen walked back in. "By the way, there's a bathroom across the hall if you need it." Derek took the opportunity to get up and stretch his legs.

When he came back in the room, Mr. Bensen looked up from his work. "Looks good. Now, here's a twist on what we've done so far. Not all payments are yearly. Sometimes a money machine will pay twice a year, or quarterly, or monthly. As long as the payments are the same and come at regular intervals, it's still an annuity. All we need to do is remember that the n in the formula is the number of payments and that we need to change r.

"Have you ever gotten a speeding ticket?"

"Uh, yeah."

"How fast were you going?"

"Uh, like 80 in a 65," Derek said with a wince.

"Like 80 what? 80 miles per minute? 80 kilometers per half hour?"

"80 miles per hour."

"Of course, but you knew you didn't need to say that, right? When you tell people you were going 80, they know you mean 80 miles per hour. Interest rates are similar. They are rates just like 80 is a rate of speed. We always quote interest rates in terms of years just like people quote speeds in miles per hour. We never say *10 percent per year,* we just say *10 percent.* So let's try two more annuities," Mr. Bensen said. "First, what is the value today of receiving $700 every six months for 27 years if the interest rate is 5%?"

Derek wrote:

$$V_0 = 700 * \frac{1 - \frac{1}{(1.025)^{54}}}{0.025} = 20,619.78$$

"Now suppose you make payments of $700 every six months for 27 years into an account that pays 5%. What is the value of the annuity exactly 27 years from today?"

Derek wrote.

$$FVA_{54} = 700 * \frac{(1.025)^{54} - 1}{0.025} = 78,229.90$$

"Perfect. Interest rates are usually quoted in APRs or annual percentage rates. Suppose a bank promised you a 10% APR on savings account deposits and you put $1,000 in. How much would you have in a year?"

"$1,100," Derek said quickly, then wrote on the board:

$$V_1 = 1,000 * 1.10^1 = 1,100.00$$

"What if the bank offered a 10% APR compounded semi-annually?" Mr. Bensen asked. "That means they pay you 5% of $1,000 or $50 in six months. Now you have $1,050 in the account. Then you get 5% of $1,050 at the end of the second six months. That's a total of $1,102.50, which is better than $1,100.00. The more frequent the compounding, the more money you make. Okay?"

"Yeah."

"Okay. Good. That's all I've got. Here's your summary and the calculator with a few problems. Next week?"

"Yes sir," said Derek and they shook hands.

STUDY PACKET:
TIME VALUE OF MONEY II

Definitions

Annual Percentage Rate—the periodic interest rate times the number of periods per year.

Annuity—a series of identical cash flows occurring at a fixed interval over a specified time period. The U.S. Securities and Exchange Commission defines annuities to include payments that are fixed, indexed, and variable. The definition may be found at the following link—http://www.sec.gov/answers/annuity.htm. For purposes of this book, annuities will be fixed.

Compounding—adding interest earned to the invested principal before calculating the new interest earned.

Growing Annuity—an annuity that increases at a given growth rate over its lifetime

Perpetuity—a series of fixed cash flows occuring at a fixed interval forever. In other words, an annuity that pays forever.

Equations

To follow is the derivation for the present value of an annuity followed by the derivation of the future value of an annuity. Notice the assumptions made in these derivations. They are extremely important.

Present Value of an Annuity

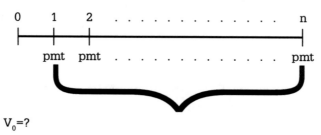

The value today of an annuity lasting n periods with the first payment made exactly one period from today is given by the following equation.

$$(3.1) \quad PVA_n = \frac{pmt}{(1+i)^1} + \frac{pmt}{(1+i)^2} + \frac{pmt}{(1+i)^3} + \cdots \frac{pmt}{(1+i)^n}$$

PVA_n is the present value of an annuity, the payment is equal to pmt, and i is the discount rate. For notational ease let $D = \frac{1}{1+i}$. Let pmt = 1. We now have:

$$PVA_n = D^1 + D^2 + D^3 + \ldots + D^n$$

Multiply both sides by D.

$$D*PVA_n = D^2 + D^3 + D^4 + \ldots + D^{n+1}$$

$$PVA_n - D^1 * PVA_n = D^1 - D^{n+1}$$

Simplifying and relaxing the assumption that pmt = 1 results in:

(3.2)
$$PVA_n = pmt * \left[\frac{1 - \frac{1}{(1+i)^n}}{i} \right]$$

In deriving equation 3.2, we assumed that the first payment would come in exactly one period from today and that there would be n payments. The payments may be made annually, quarterly, monthly, or at any other fixed interval. The interest rate, i, must match the frequency of the payments. In other words, if the payments are made annually then i is an annual rate, and if the payments are made monthly then i is a monthly rate.

PVA_n is called the present value of the annuity. The term *present value* should not be taken literally. The result of equation 3.2 is not the value of the payments today except when the payments begin exactly one period from today. The result of equation 3.2 should be interpreted as the value of the payments one period before they begin, regardless of when the first payment occurs.

Example 1. What would an investor pay today to receive $1,000 per year for 12 years with the first payment made six years from today? Assume an interest rate of 10%.

One could discount each cash flow as shown in Chapter 2.

$$V_0 = \frac{1,000}{1.10^6} + \frac{1,000}{1.10^7} + \frac{1,000}{1.10^8} + \frac{1,000}{1.10^9} + \frac{1,000}{1.10^{10}} + \frac{1,000}{1.10^{11}}$$
$$+ \frac{1,000}{1.10^{12}} + \frac{1,000}{1.10^{13}} + \frac{1,000}{1.10^{14}} + \frac{1,000}{1.10^{15}} + \frac{1,000}{1.10^{16}} + \frac{1,000}{1.10^{17}}$$

This is a long and painful way to find the answer. Annuities of 360 payments are common. A shortcut is helpful.

Treat this question as a two-step problem. First, use the present value annuity formula to find the value of the annuity in year 5.

$$V_s = 1,000 * [\frac{1 - \frac{1}{(1.10)^{12}}}{0.10}] = 6,813.69$$

Since the payments begin in year 6, equation 3.2 may be used to find the value in year 5. You are indifferent as to whether you receive $6,813.69 five years from today or the annuity that begins in year 6. The question now becomes, what is the value today of receiving $6,813.69 five years from today? We know this answer from Chapter 2.

$$V_0 = \frac{V_s}{(1+i)^5} = \frac{6,813.69}{1.10^5} = 4,230.77$$

Future Value of an Annuity

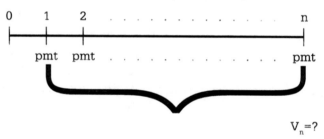

Assume a payment is deposited into an account every period for n consecutive periods with the first deposit being made exactly one period from today. The value of the account immediately after the last payment is made is called the future value of the annuity and given by the following equation:

$$(3.3)\ FVA_n = pmt*(1+i)^0 + pmt*(1+i)^1 + pmt*(1+i)^2 + pmt*(1+i)^{n-1}$$

For notational ease let D = (1 + i) and pmt = 1.

$$FVA_n = D^0 + D^1 + D^2 + \dots + D^{n-1}$$

$$D * FVA_n = D^1 + D^2 + D^3 + \ldots + D^n$$

$$D * FVA_n - FVA_n = D^n - D^0$$

Simplifying and relaxing the assumption that pmt = 1 results in:

(3.4) $$FVA_n = pmt * \frac{(1 + i)^n - 1}{i}$$

FVA_n is called the future value of the annuity. The term *future value* is incomplete. It does not identify the exact future date. The result of equation 3.4 is the value of the payments immediately following the final payment.

Example 2. Assume you deposit $1,000 into an account every year for 13 years with the first deposit being made exactly five years from today. Assume the account earns 10%. What is the value of the account 25 years from today?

This is a two-step problem. First, use equation 3.4 to find the value of the annuity immediately following the final deposit, which is made in year 17.

$$V_{17} = 1,000 * \frac{1.10^{13} - 1}{0.10} = 24,522.71$$

From Chapter 2 we know:

$$V_{25} = V_{17} * (1 + i)^8 = 24,522.71 * 1.10^8 = 52,566.61$$

Perpetuities

A perpetuity is an annuity that pays forever. Look back at equation 3.2. If there are an infinite number of payments then n must equal infinity. Letting n approach infinity results in:

(3.5)
$$PV_{perpetuity} = \frac{pmt}{i}$$

Present value is still not literally the value today. It is the value of the perpetuity one period before the payments begin.

Growing Annuity

Imagine an annuity with cash flows that grow at a constant rate. For example, assume you are promised a four-year annuity. The first payment will be $1,000 and paid next year. Unlike a normal annuity the payment will increase by 10% every year. So, you will receive $1,000, then $1,100, then $1,210, and finally $1,331. The long way to value this cash flow stream is

$$V_0 = \frac{1,000}{1.05^1} + \frac{1,100}{1.05^2} + \frac{1,210}{1.05^3} + \frac{1,331}{1.05^4}$$

The general equation is as follows.

$$V_0 = \frac{pmt}{(1+r)^1} + \frac{pmt(1+g)^1}{(1+r)^2} + \frac{pmt(1+g)^2}{(1+r)^3} + ... + \frac{pmt(1+g)^{n-1}}{(1+r)^n}$$

To simplify multiply both sides by $\frac{1+r}{1+g}$. Then take the difference of the two equations and simplify. The result is:

(3.6)
$$V_0 = \frac{pmt}{r-g}\left[1 - \frac{(1+g)^n}{(1+r)^n}\right]$$

Here *pmt* is the initial payment, *r* is the discount rate, *g* is the growth rate of the payment, and *n* is the number of payments. Notice that this equation 3.6, much like equation 3.2, was derived assuming the next payment occurred one period from today. Therefore, equation 3.6 results in the value of a growing annuity one period before the payments start. What if the payments continued forever? Find the equation for the present value of a growing perpetuity. We'll come back to this concept in Chapter 7.

We can also find the future value of a growing annuity. The appropriate equation is

(3.7)
$$V_n = pmt\left[\frac{(1+r)^n - (1+g)^n}{r-g}\right]$$

Remember that future value means the value on the day the final payment is made.

Compounding Frequency

Up to this point we have considered only annual cash flows and annual compounding. Annual compounding means we calculate interest earned and add it to the principal balance once per year.

For example, suppose you deposit $1,000 into an account paying 10%. In three years the value is not $1,000 + 100 + 100 + 100 = $1,300. The interest rate is not applied only to the $1,000 deposit each year. Rather, interest is added to the principal after each year.

$$V_1 = 1,000*1.10 = 1,100$$

$$V_2 = 1,100*1.10 = 1,210$$

$$V_3 = 1,210*1.10 = 1,331$$

Suppose a bank offers to pay 10% on a savings account and compounds semi-annually.

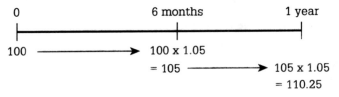

Suppose Bank A offered a 10% APR compounded semi-annually while Bank B offered a 9.8% APR compounded monthly. To make a valid comparison between the two banks find the effective annual rate, EAR:

(3.8) $$EAR = (1 + \frac{APR}{m})^m - 1$$

where m is the compounding frequency.

For semi-annual compounding, m equals 2; for monthly compounding m equals 12, etc. As the compounding frequency increases, m gets larger and the EAR increases. Compounding can be done daily, hourly, or even continuously. While considering continuous compounding, Jacob Bernoulli discovered the constant $e = 2.71828$. ... Formally:

(3.9) $$e = \lim_{m \to \infty}(1 + \frac{1}{m})^m$$

Therefore, assuming continuous compounding:

(3.10) $$FV = PV\, e^{rT}$$

And:

(3.11) $$EAR = e^r - 1$$

Loan Amortization

Suppose you borrow $15,000 to buy a car. You are to make the same monthly payment for 12 months. The APR on the loan was 6.00%. The payment schedule is shown on the next page.

Month	Beginning Balance	Payment	Principal	Interest	Ending Balance
January	15,000.00	1,291.00	1,216.00	75.00	13,784.00
February	13,784.00	1,291.00	1,222.08	68.92	12,561.93
March	12,561.93	1,291.00	1,228.19	62.81	11,333.74
April	11,333.74	1,291.00	1,234.33	56.67	10,099.41
May	10,099.41	1,291.00	1,240.50	50.50	8,858.91
June	8,858.91	1,291.00	1,246.70	44.29	7,612.21
July	7,612.21	1,291.00	1,252.94	38.06	6,359.28
August	6,359.28	1,291.00	1,259.20	31.80	5,100.08
September	5,100.08	1,291.00	1,265.50	25.50	3,834.58
October	3,834.58	1,291.00	1,271.82	19.17	2,562.76
November	2,562.76	1,291.00	1,278.18	12.81	1,284.57
December	1,284.57	1,291.00	1,284.57	6.42	0.00

When the loan is initiated the payment is determined using the equation:

$$PVA_n = pmt * \left[\frac{1 - \frac{1}{(1 + i)^n}}{i} \right]$$

$$15,000 = pmt * \left[\frac{1 - \frac{1}{(1 + 0.06/12)^{12}}}{0.06/12} \right]$$

So pmt = 1,291.00. Part of the payment of 1,291.00 is interest. The remainder goes to reduce the outstanding balance of the loan. The interest portion is equal to the outstanding balance times the interest rate.

The January interest payment is:

$$15,000.00 * 0.06/12 = 75.00.$$

The January principal payment is:

$$1,291.00 - 75.00 = 1,216.00.$$

The February interest payment is:

$$13,784.00 * 0.06/12 = 68.92.$$

The February principal payment is:

$$1,291.00 - 68.92 = 1,222.08.$$

Mortgages work in a similar fashion. They are typically amortized for 15 or 30 years.

The Calculator

A financial calculator will make solving the problem set for this and future chapters much quicker and easier. However, to arrive at correct answers, one must understand the equations programmed into the financial calculator. It is best to work problems without the aid of a financial calculator until a thorough understanding of the equations has been achieved.

Two popular financial calculators are the Texas Instruments BAII Plus and the HP 10II+. Both calculators are programmed to solve equations 3.2 and 3.4.

This book assumes readers are using the Texas Instruments model and will give directions on how to use it. The HP is similar. The instruction manual accompanying the HP should be sufficient to allow the reader to use it as well.

First, make sure the calculator has the proper settings. For the Texas Instruments calculator do the following:

- Press '2ⁿᵈ' then 'Format' then '9' then 'ENTER'. This will tell the calculator to display the exact answer or the answer up to 9 decimal places.
- Press '2ⁿᵈ' then 'P/Y' then '1' then 'ENTER'. This will tell the calculator that the payment frequency will be once per year. Keep P/Y = 1 regardless of the payment frequency. It is easier to adjust 'n' and 'I/Y' than it is to constantly change 'P/Y'.
- Press '2ⁿᵈ' then 'SET'. If 'BGN' appears then press '2ⁿᵈ' then 'ENTER'. 'END' will appear. Leave the calculator in 'END' mode.

Example 3. What would an investor pay today to receive $1,000 per year for 12 years with the first payment made one year from today? Assume an interest rate of 10%.

- Press '12' then 'N'; press '10' then 'I/Y'; press '1,000' then 'PMT'; press '0' then 'FV'. Finally, press 'CPT' then 'PV'. The result will be '-6,813.691823'. Note the inputs may be entered in any order.

Don't worry about the negative sign in the result. Think of positive numbers as cash you receive and negative numbers as cash you pay. The negative simply means you pay $6,813.69 rather than receive it. If one party is receiving cash then the counterparty in the transition is paying cash.

After completing each problem, press '2ⁿᵈ' then 'CLR TVM'. This will clear the calculator's memory so information from a previous question will not be considered in the current question.

Example 4. Assume you deposit $1,000 into an account every year for 13 years with the first deposit being made exactly one year from today. Assume the account earns 10%. What is the value of the account 13 years from today?

- Press '13' then 'N'; press '10' then 'I/Y'; press '0' then 'PV'; press '1000' then 'PMT'. Finally, press 'CPT' then 'FV'. The result will be -24,522.71214.

Concluding Remarks

The topics covered in this Study Packet have application to many different specific issues in Finance. Be sure to work each problem. This problem set is designed to teach as well as test.

PROBLEM SET

1. What is the value today of a money machine that will pay $1,000 per year for 20 years? Assume the first payment is made one year from today and the interest rate is 7%.
2. What is the value today of a money machine that will pay $1,000 per year for 20 years? Assume the first payment is made five years from today and the interest rate is 7%.
3. What is the value today of a money machine that will pay $1,000 per year for 20 years? Assume the first payment is made five years from today and the interest rate is 9%.
4. Of the money machines in questions 1-3 which one is the most valuable? Notice the effect of size, timing, and risk. Since the money machine in #3 has the highest interest rate it must be the riskiest. More details about risk will be covered in Chapter 6.
5. What is the value today of a money machine that will pay $500 every six months for 20 years? Assume the first payment is made six months from today and the interest rate is 7%.
6. What is the value today of a money machine that will pay $500 every six months for 20 years? Assume the first payment is made five years from today and the interest rate is 7%.
7. What is the value today of a money machine that will pay $500 every six months for 20 years? Assume the first payment is made five years from today and the interest rate is 9%.
8. Of the money machines in question 1 and 7 which one is the most valuable? Notice that both make the same total payments over 20 years.
9. What is the value today of a money machine that will pay $2,000 per year for 10 years? Assume the first payment is made today and that there are 10 total payments. The interest rate is 8%.
10. Should Derek take the following deal? Bensen will pay him $3,000 per year for 20 years with the first payment to be made

today and the last payment to be made 19 years from today. In exchange, he must pay Bensen $46,000 exactly five years from today. Assume an interest rate of 9%.

Future Value of an Annuity

11. Derek will deposit $700 per year for 10 years into an account that earns 7%. The first deposit is made next year. How much will be in the account 10 years from today?
12. Derek will deposit $700 per year for 11 years into an account that earns 7%. The first deposit is made today. How much will be in the account 10 years from today?
13. Derek will deposit $2,000 per year for 15 years into an account that earns 9%. The first deposit is made next year. How much will be in the account 20 years from today?
14. Repeat #13 assuming that Derek has $10,000 in the account today.
15. Derek will deposit $1,700 per year for 13 years into an account that earns 10%. Assuming the first deposit is made 8 years from today, how much will be in the account 30 years from today?

Perpetuities

16. What is the value today of receiving $1,500 per year forever? Assume the first payment is made next year and the discount rate is 10%.
17. Repeat #16 but assume the first payment is made four years from today.
18. If you are willing to pay $25,000 today to receive $2,000 per year forever then your required rate of return must be ____%. Assume the first payment is received one year from today.

19. If you are willing to pay $30,000 today to receive a perpetuity with the first payment occurring next year then the payment must be $_____. Assume a 5% discount rate.

20. What discount rate would make you indifferent between receiving $1,500 per year forever and $2,500 per year for 20 years? Assume the first payment of both cash flow streams occurs in one year.

Retirement Problems

One of the major uses of the concepts covered in this chapter is to assist people with retirement planning. The following questions will demonstrate this.

For questions 21 - 25 assume that today is Derek's 25th birthday.

21. Derek has been advised that he needs to have $3,000,000 in his retirement account the day he turns 65. He estimates his retirement account will pay 7% interest. How much does he need to have in the account today if he wants to make no future contributions to the account? Next, assume he chooses not to deposit anything today. Rather he chooses to make annual deposits into the retirement account starting on his 26th birthday and ending on his 65th birthday. How much must those deposits be?

22. Derek can deposit $12,000 on each birthday beginning with his 26th and ending with his 65th. What will the rate on the retirement account need to be for him to have $3,000,000 in it when he retires on his 65th birthday?

23. If Derek plans to deposit $12,000 into his retirement account on each birthday beginning with his 26th and the account earns 7%, how long will it take him to accumulate $3,000,000?

24. Derek has second thoughts about needing $3,000,000 at retirement. He decides that he needs $100,000 per year in retirement to cover his living expenses. Therefore, he wants to withdraw

$100,000 on each birthday from his 66th to his 85th. How much will he need in his retirement account on his 65th birthday? Assume a interest rate of 7%.

25. Derek still plans to retire on his 65th birthday. However, he plans to work part-time until his 70th birthday. If this is the case he will be able to make contributions to his retirement account from his 26th birthday to his 65th birthday. He will not need to make withdrawals until his 71st birthday. If he needs $3,000,000 in the account on his 71st birthday, what must the contributions be? Assume a 7% interest rate.

26. Derek still plans to retire on his 65th birthday. However, he plans to work part-time until his 70th birthday. If this is the case he will be able to make contributions to his retirement account from his 26th birthday to his 65th birthday. He will not need to make withdrawals until his 71st birthday. He plans to withdraw $100,000 on each birthday from his 71st to his 90th. How much must his contributions to the retirement account be to achieve his goal? Assume a 7% interest rate.

Compounding Frequency

27. A bank offers 4.00% on savings accounts. What is the effective annual rate if interest is compounded semi-annually? Quarterly? Monthly? Daily? Continuously?

28. Assume a bank offers an effective annual rate of 5.20%. If compounding is quarterly what is the APR?

Loan Amortization

29. Derek borrows $200,000 to buy a house. He has a 30-year mortgage with a rate of 6.00%. The monthly mortgage payment is $_____.

30. Use information in #29. After making 100 payments, Derek sells the house for $220,000. How much must he pay the mortgage holder?

31. Derek borrows $30,000 to buy a car. He will make monthly payments for 6 years. The car loan has an interest rate of 5%. What will the payments be?

32. Use information in #31. After a year Derek decides to pay off his car loan. How much must he give the bank?

33. Derek decides to buy a new car. The dealership offers him a choice of paying $500 per month for 5 years (with the first payment due next month) or paying $27,000 today. Assume a 4% discount rate. Which option should he choose?

34. What discount rate in #33 would make Derek indifferent between the options?

35. Derek plans to buy a $36,000 car. The dealership offers zero percent financing for 48 months with the first payment due at signing (today). Derek would be willing to pay for the car in full today if the dealership offers him $____ cash back. Assume a 5% interest rate.

Additional Problems

There is no limit to the way financial transactions can be structured. It is important for a financial analyst to understand the value of any potential cash flow stream. Questions 36–50 present unusual and challenging situations.

36. Derek wants to withdraw $10,000 from his account five years from today and $12,000 from his account 10 years from today. He currently has $2,000 in the account. How much must he deposit each year for the next 10 years? Assume a 6% interest rate.

37. Derek currently has $10,000 in an account that pays 5%. He will with draw $5,000 every other year beginning next year and ending in year 9. He will deposit $10,000 every other year beginning two years from todayand ending in year 10. How much will be in the account 20 years from today?

38. Derek can deposit $100 per month for the next 10 years into an account at Bank A. The first deposit will be made next month. Bank A pays 12% and compounds interest monthly. Derek can deposit $1,200 per year for the next 10 years into an account at Bank B. The first deposit will be made next year. Bank B compounds interest annually. What rate must Bank B pay for Derek to have the same amount in both accounts after 10 years?

39. Money Machine A pays $2,000 per year for 10 years. Money Machine B pays $20,000 five years from today. Which machine is more valuable? Assume an interest rate of 7%.

40. Does the interest rate in #39 matter?

41. You are considering loaning Caspian Sea Drinks $250,000. You require a 6% rate of return. Caspian Sea Drinks must promise to make equal payments of $_____ per year over the next 10 years in order for you to make the loan. The first payment will be made one year from today.

42. Which loan has the lower interest rate? Loan A is for $100,000 and will be repaid in 5 annual payments of $23,000 with the first payment made next year. Loan B is for $225,000 and will be repaid in seven annual installments of $40,000 with the first payment made next year.

43. Assume today is your 25th birthday and you make a $10,000 deposit in your retirement account. You will make a deposit on each birthday until you are 65. You plan to increase the amount of the deposits by 3% each year. If the account earns 8% then how much will you have in the account on your 65th birthday.

44. What is the value today of receiving the following growing annuity? The first payment of $1,000 is made next year. The payments

increase by 5% per year until the final payment is made 20 years from today. The appropriate discount rate is 10%.

45. Assume today is your 35th birthday. On your 71st birthday you plan on making the first withdrawal from your retirement account. The withdrawal will be $125,000 and the withdrawals on your following birthdays will increase by 2% per year. The final withdrawal will be on your 91st birthday. In order to achieve this goal you will begin today by making a deposit into your retirement account and the deposits on your following birthdays will increase by 3%. The final deposit will be made on your 65th birthday. You will then retire and work part-time until you begin to withdraw from the account on your 71st birthday. The account is project to earn 7%. What must today's deposit be?

46. You can choose between receiving $300,000 today or the following growing annuity. You will receive 25 payments. The first payment is made 5 years from today and will be $10,000. The payments will grow by 10% per year. Your required rate of return is 6%. Should you choose the lump sum or the annuity?

47. Assume you are willing to pay $8,000 today for a money machine that generates the following cash flows: $1,000 per year for five years with the first payment made next year plus an unknown payment beginning in year six that continues forever. Assume an interest rate of 6%. What must the unknown payments be?

48. Assume you are willing to pay $100,000 today to receive $10,000 per year for 10 years with the first payment to be made next year plus $13,000 per year forever with the first payment made 11 years from today. What is your required rate of return?

49. You are considering selling your share of a business you started with two brothers. You believe your share is worth $5 million. The brothers offer you the following (1) $500,000 today. (2) A 5 year growing annuity with the first payment of $500,000 to be made next year. The annuity will grow at 4%. (3) A $1,000,000 one-time payment five years from today. (4) $750,000 per year

forever with the first payment made six years from today. Your required rate of return is 15%. Should you take the offer? Why?

50. Use the information in #49. Assume all terms are set except today's payment. What is minimum payment must the brothers make to you to make you accept the deal?

3.1

For the third Wednesday straight, the bench in the park was empty until Derek and Moss sat on it.

"He's a movie buff," Derek said.

Moss said nothing.

"He quoted *Pulp Fiction* and some musical—*Mary Poppins* or something."

Moss stared at Derek for a few seconds. "Is that really all you've got to tell me?"

"Yeah," Derek said. "It was that and Finance stuff."

Moss sat back on the bench, stuck his legs out, put his hands behind his head and looked up through the leaves. He let out a long slow sigh then sat, silent, for a long minute.

Derek sat back too. It was awkward. He knew Moss was disappointed that he wasn't telling him anything. He also knew Moss had been trained to accomplish things and that he was probably trying to accomplish something in Derek now using dramatic silence. But he didn't feel bad. He was eager to process what he'd learned from Mr. Bensen and do some homework.

Finally, Moss slowly straightened up. He bent forward, rested his elbows on his knees, and turned toward Derek. As he talked, he looked mostly at his own hands, locked together at the fingers, which he flexed every few seconds. "I gave you that *hero* speech last week because I believe it, and I want you to believe it too. I want you to be motivated by that. But the fact is, you've gotta perform or our arrangement is going to have to change. I don't mind if you tell me you tried this or that and it didn't work, but when you come talking about *Mary Poppins*, I feel like you're mocking me."

"*My Fair Lady*!" Derek said. "That's what it was."

Moss clenched his fingers together and continued, "You're getting paid right? Not by us—the government can't pay you—but by Stovall." Moss looked up at Derek.

"No," Derek said.

"You said you were."

"Last week I told you I'd gone by the office and set everything up—which I have. But I haven't seen any money."

"Check your balance now."

"I don't have a smartphone."

"Are you kidding? Here." Moss pulled out his phone, navigated to a web browser, and handed it to Derek. Derek took it and fumbled around until he'd logged in and checked his account activity.

"Whoa," Derek said, and sat up straight. A $10,000 deposit had been made in the last hour.

Moss sat up too. "Okay. So. You're getting paid. Stovall's paying you. Don't worry about what it's for. I told you before—Stovall's an idiot. He's an idiot, but he's not a criminal like Bensen. The government can't pay you, but I've arranged this payment through Stovall, as a bonus to you. I know this is hard for you and it's asking a lot. But it's not like you're not getting any compensation."

"But—" Derek started to talk.

"No. Listen. Go shopping. Get yourself a new phone. Think about your assignment and make an effort. That's all I'm asking. Make an effort. Please don't come back here next week and talk to me about movies." Moss stood up and left the park.

—

Derek didn't buy a new phone. He didn't buy anything. He got home, checked his account again, saw the money, and thought. After classes the next day he went to the bank and opened a savings account and shifted all of the Stovall money into it. He didn't have a plan. He just knew he didn't feel right spending that money—not yet anyway. He had things to spend it on—things he needed, things he wanted, student loans—but something felt wrong about it. He couldn't tell if he didn't trust Stovall and Moss, or if he didn't want to spend the money because that would obligate him to put more effort into getting the Caspian Sea ingredients.

The way Moss saw it, the payment obligated him. But Derek thought, "If I don't benefit from the payment, I'm not gonna feel bad about not *earning* it. If it's in savings I can give it all back, plus a little bit of interest, any time. If for some reason Mr. Bensen writes down the ingredients on a piece of paper and hands it to me, then I keep the money." Based on Moss's last conversation, what he wanted was proof that Derek had "made an effort." That's what Derek had to do—prove to Moss that he'd made an effort.

—

This time when Derek got to the conference room, the door was closed. He looked in the long, thin vertical window and saw Mr. Bensen standing at the window, arms crossed, looking out toward the neighboring buildings. He looked deep in thought. Derek didn't want to disturb him. *But if he's in here, he's waiting for me. Why else would he be here?* Derek checked his watch. *One minute early. Maybe I should go to the bathroom, and when I come back, he'll be sitting, ready for me—maybe the door'll be open. But then he might think I'm getting here late. Late isn't good.*

Derek looked at Mr. Bensen. He couldn't see his face, but he could see his left ear; it appeared to twitch. Derek studied his view of Mr. Bensen's head for a few seconds, then gasped and jumped back from the window. He had caught the reflection of Mr. Bensen's face in the window and their eyes met.

Derek hadn't been doing anything wrong, but the realization that Mr. Bensen had been watching him looking in the window, combined with the look on Mr. Bensen's face, shocked Derek. He went across the hall into the bathroom and stood at the sink and rinsed his face. He tried to understand what he'd seen. *What was that face? Maybe it was just because it was a reflection in the window. Sinister. I don't think I've ever used that word, but that's what it was. It was a grin, but a sinister grin.* He splashed his face again. *How do I know what a sinister grin looks like? Moss. He has a sinister grin, but he's an agent—he's supposed to. Maybe I should have a sinister grin. If I had a sinister grin, maybe I could earn that $10,000 and be a hero like Moss said. Do heroes have sinister grins?* Derek tried to give himself a sinister grin in the mirror.

Derek dried his face, composed himself as much as possible, and walked back across the hall. The door was open. Mr. Bensen stood up from the table when Derek walked in the room. "So, what's new?" Mr. Bensen asked.

Sinister, Derek thought. They shook hands and Derek swallowed and said, "Not much."

CHAPTER 4

FINANCIAL STATEMENTS:
THE LIFEBLOOD OF MAGIC MONEY MACHINES

M r. Bensen stepped up to the whiteboard, picked up a marker and wrote *Financial Statements* at the top of the board. "We're gonna start with the *Balance Sheet* and *Income Statement*," he said. "You know anything about those?"

"I should, but I don't. I mean I know they're financial."

"No worries. We'll start simple," Mr. Bensen said and sat down. Derek searched Mr. Bensen's face for whatever he'd seen before, but he saw nothing scary. Mr. Bensen didn't seem any different. Derek gradually relaxed and focused on the material instead of the face in the window. "Remember the story. When we first formed Caspian Sea Drinks, LLC we had three owners: Spencer, Alex and me. Justin and Stovall were the bondholders. We were selling a lot of product but we made one big mistake that almost cost us the company. We had financial statements but we didn't have a clue about what they were telling us. It can get complicated, but when we first started they were simple. However, simple as they were, I still managed to mess things up. I'm telling you the stuff I should've known when I got started. Who knows when you'll need it?

"Any business needs to know how much money it's making—the *Income Statement*—what it owns and what it owes—the *Balance Sheet*—and where the cash is coming from and going to—the

Statement of Cash Flows. Income Statement first. Here are the ones we showed the angel investors."

Income Statement 12-31-1997	
Sales	70,000
COGS	17,500
Gross profit	52,500
Operating expenses	27,500
Depreciation	3,000
Operating profit	22,000
Interest expense	1,000
EBT	21,000
Taxes	8,400
Net Income	12,600

Income Statement 12-31-1998	
Sales	100,000
COGS	25,000
Gross profit	75,000
Operating expenses	45,000
Depreciation	3,000
Operating profit	27,000
Interest expense	1,000
EBT	26,000
Taxes	10,400
Net Income	15,600

"And here are the definitions of each category," Mr. Bensen said and handed Derek another sheet of paper. You have to memorize them and the order they come in. *Depreciation* is a little different from the rest. For all the others Caspian Sea either gets money or pays money. We get money from our customers—that's *Sales*. We pay for the ingredients—that's *Cost of Goods Sold*. But before we calculate our taxes we get to subtract *Depreciation*. We don't write a check for depreciation, we just subtract it from our earnings and then calculate the taxes we owe."

"So this *Net Income* line isn't literally the amount of money you made?" Derek asked.

"Right. That's why we need a *Statement of Cash Flows*. We'll do that later. What do these *Income Statements* tell you? Is Caspian Sea a good business? Would you invest?

"Yeah. Yes. Looks good to me. You're making money and increasing sales."

"Okay. Now let's tackle the *Balance Sheet*. What did we own? Who and what did we owe?" Mr. Bensen asked.

Derek had to think. "Let's see. In the beginning? You said you had that cart. You probably had some other equipment; coolers and stuff. And you had some juice—product—already made. And some cash in the bank?"

"Good. You're only missing one of our assets. Now who do we owe?"

"Spencer and, uh, what's his ... Stovall." As always, Derek tried to distance himself from any awareness of Stovall.

"The bondholders."

"Yeah. And did you have any employees then? You'd probably owe them something. I can't think of anyone else."

"No. Not bad. Take a look at these old *Balance Sheets*." Mr. Bensen handed Derek another sheet. "This is about as basic as it gets."

Balance Sheet 12-31-1997

Cash	40,000	Notes payable	0
Accounts receivable	20,000	Accounts payable	2,000
Inventory	25,000	Accruals	1,000
Current Assets	**85,000**	Current portion LTD	0
Gross fixed assets	80,000	**Current Liabilities**	**3,000**
Accumulated depreciation	4,000	Long-term debt	110,000
Net fixed assets	76,000	Preferred stock	0
Total Assets	**161,000**	Common stock	47,000
		Retained earnings	1,000
		Total Liabilities & Equity	**161,000**

Balance Sheet 12-31-1998

Cash	33,000	Notes payable	0
Accounts receivable	22,000	Accounts payable	2,000
Inventory	35,600	Accruals	1,000
Current Assets	**90,600**	Current portion LTD	110,000
Gross fixed assets	93,000	**Current Liabilities**	**113,000**
Accumulated depreciation	7,000	Long-term debt	0
Net fixed assets	86,000	Preferred stock	0
Total Assets	**176,600**	Common stock	47,000
		Retained earnings	16,600
		Total Liabilities & Equity	**176,600**

"Earlier when you were listing our assets you didn't include *Accounts Receivable* which you didn't know about. Occasionally a local barbecue place would cater lunches for different groups and we would supply Caspian Sea. In those cases, we would deliver the drinks and leave a bill. We'd usually get paid in thirty days or less. That's not cash but it soon will be."

"Okay," Derek said looking over the sheet. "But I don't see the cart and equipment anywhere? And what is *Accumulated Depreciation*?

"Here's a list of definitions for the different entries." Mr. Bensen handed Derek another sheet. "Memorize them and memorize the way the *Balance Sheet* is set up. Here's the big picture. On one side of the *Balance Sheet* you have a list of stuff you own—the *Assets*. On the other you have a list of what you owe—the *Liabilities*. The difference between those two numbers is the *Book Value* of the company—the *Equity*. Judging by the *Balance Sheet* only, is Caspian Sea a good company? Would you invest? Say you're one of the potential angel investors. What do you think?"

"I'm ... I don't know."

"You need a better feel for what it's telling you. First, get the fundamentals down. Take this info and construct an *Income Statement* and *Balance Sheet*. Take your time, get it right, then practice until you can do it in your sleep."

"Build my instincts," Derek said.

"There you go. Get started. I'll be back in a few." Mr. Bensen stood and walked out. Derek went to work.

Assignment 1

Construct an *Income Statement* and *Balance Sheet* from the following list of items. [See page 105.]

Mr. Bensen walked back in a few minutes later, with a calculator. "Okay. Let's see. You looked at the two *Income Statements* and said you would invest. You said sales were up and Caspian Sea was making money. You were right. You didn't mention that cost of goods sold and operating expenses were up as well."

"I kind of thought that was a given. If we're selling more stuff, then expenses should be higher."

"Yeah, but how much higher? Look at these." Mr. Bensen gave Derek two more sheets and the calculator.

Income Statement 12-31-1997	
Sales	100.0%
COGS	25.0%
Gross profit	75.0%
Operating expenses	39.3%
Depreciation	4.3%
Operating profit	31.4%
Interest expense	1.4%
EBT	30.0%
Taxes	12.0%
Net Income	18.0%

Income Statement 12-31-1998	
Sales	100.0%
COGS	25.0%
Gross profit	75.0%
Operating expenses	45.0%
Depreciation	3.0%
Operating profit	27.0%
Interest expense	1.0%
EBT	26.0%
Taxes	10.4%
Net Income	15.6%

"These are *Common-sized Income Statements*," Mr. Bensen said. Take each number in the *Income Statement* and divide by sales. Now we can see if the company is really doing better or not. *COGS* didn't change as a percentage of sales. Operating expenses did. That tells me there is a problem. Net income dropped in percentage terms. It was 18.0%, now it's 15.6%. There may be trouble on Caspian Sea, huh? We can do the same thing with *Balance Sheets*. Take a look at this." Mr. Bensen gave Derek two more sheets.

Balance Sheet 12-31-1997

Cash	24.8%	Notes payable	0.0%
Accounts receivable	12.4%	Accounts payable	1.2%
Inventory	15.5%	Accruals	0.6%
Current Assets	**52.8%**	Current portion LTD	0.0%
Gross fixed assets	49.7%	**Current Liabilities**	**1.9%**
Accumulated depreciation	2.5%	Long-term debt	68.3%
Net fixed assets	47.2%	Preferred stock	0.0%
Total Assets	**100.0%**	Common stock	29.2%
		Retained earnings	0.6%
		Total Liabilities & Equity	**100.0%**

Balance Sheet 12-31-1998

Cash	18.7%	Notes payable	0.0%
Accounts receivable	12.5%	Accounts payable	1.1%
Inventory	20.2%	Accruals	0.6%
Current Assets	**51.3%**	Current portion LTD	62.3%
Gross fixed assets	52.7%	**Current Liabilities**	**64.0%**
Accumulated depreciation	4.0%	Long-term debt	0.0%
Net fixed assets	48.7%	Preferred stock	0.0%
Total Assets	**100.0%**	Common stock	26.6%
		Retained earnings	9.4%
		Total Liabilities & Equity	**100.0%**

"Potential investors would look at the *Common-sized Income Statements* and *Balance Sheets* and notice that operating expenses were going up too fast," Mr. Bensen said. They could look at the *Balance Sheet* and see that inventory was up.

"Imagine an investor is looking to get into a specific industry like beverage producers. Some beverage makers are large like Coca-Cola and some are small like us. A potential investor would do two things with *Common-sized Financial Statements.*

"First, she would compare the financials for Caspian Sea over time. That's called a *Time Series Comparison.* Next, she would compare the *Common-sized Financials* of the different firms in the same years. That's called a *Cross-sectional Comparison.* This allows investors to spot strengths and weaknesses after adjusting for size."

"Why did you say *she?*" Derek asked.

"Welcome to the 21st Century," was Mr. Bensen's answer.

Assignment 2

Construct the *Common-sized Income Statement* and *Balance Sheet* using the information from Assignment 1.

"There's more to analyzing financials than just looking at *Common-sized Statements.* Now let's talk about financial ratios. Remember Natasha?"

"The swimmer. How could I forget Natasha?"

"Yeah. Watch yourself. Remember about relationships. Your last two comments would've been deal breakers with many of my colleagues."

"Sorry," Derek said.

"Don't apologize—learn. Now, Natasha has a reputation to protect. Before she lets the angel investors listen to our pitch, she wants to make sure Caspian Sea has a good shot at making it. She wants to know why we need money, what we plan to do with it, and if that plan will work. To assess all of that, she calculates these ratios. They fall into four categories, 1) *Profitability*, 2) *Liquidity*, 3) *Asset Utilization*, and 4) *Debt Utilization*.

"Here's a sheet with details and formulas to calculate the ratios. Calculate them, try not to be a chauvinist, and I'll be back in a minute."

Derek did the work quickly. Mr. Bensen walked back in five minutes later.

Liquidity ratios	1997	1998
Current ratio	28.33	0.80
Quick ratio	20.00	0.49
Asset Utilization		
Avg collection period	102.86	79.20
Inventory turnover	0.70	0.70
Inv conversion period	514.29	512.64
Total asset turnover	0.43	0.57
Payables period	41.14	28.80
Debt Utilization		
Debt ratio	0.702	0.640
Times interest earned	22.000	27.000
Profitability		
ROA	7.83%	8.83%
ROE	26.25%	24.53%
Gross profit margin	75.00%	75.00%
Operating profit margin	31.43%	27.00%
Net profit margin	18.00%	15.60%

"Alright. Looks good. We could spend weeks going through each number and talking about what it means. For now, just look at one or two. Our big problem was obvious. Look at the current ratio. We had more in liabilities that were about to come due than we had in cash and things we could turn into cash quickly."

"Question," Derek interrupted. "If the current ratio is above 1, does that mean you're okay?"

"Good question. Sometimes, but not necessarily. It depends on the type of business you're in. Any financial analyst will know that firms in a particular industry need a current ratio above some number, say 2.

"Natasha looked at these numbers and saw why we came to her for money. We had $110,000 principal payment coming up and only $33,000 in cash. She saw the problem with rising expenses but also saw that we had a good profit margin. Caspian Sea Drinks had problems, but those problems could be fixed. Without taking a drink, Natasha was convinced we had a good product and that we were worthy candidates for her angel investors.

"What about the *Statement of Cash Flows*? Didn't she ask for that?"

"Yeah," Mr. Bensen said and checked his watch. "You're right. That was very important. Next time we'll talk about that and about making *Pro-forma Financials*. Right now, I've gotta run. Here's your stuff for next week," he said, and then stood up and walked out of the office without a handshake.

Assignment 3

Calculate ratios using the information in Assignment 1.

ASSIGNMENTS

Many of the minor details of constructing the financial statements are left to financial statement analysis textbooks. The goal of this chapter is to give the reader a general view of the *Income Statement* and *Balance Sheet* and to develop a sense of the role they play in a firm's financial decision making. After developing this basic skill set, the interested reader may continue to more advanced and realistic textbooks.

Definitions

COGS—cost of goods sold.

Gross profit—sales revenue minus COGS.

Operating expenses—expenses incurred during the course of running the firm. These expenses include salaries, advertising expenses, maintenance costs, research and development costs, lease payments, and general and administrative expenses.

Depreciation—the decline in value of plants and equipment. Depreciation is deducted from earnings for tax purposes but is not an actual cash flow. Depreciation must be calculated per IRS rules but for simplicity this book will only use straight-line depreciation as discussed in Chapter 9. Depreciation is included in COGS for manufacturers and in operating expenses for retailers. This text will list depreciation as a separate line item after operating expenses.

EBIT—earnings before interest and taxes.

NI—net income. Also referred to as net earnings and net profits. The terms *income*, *earnings*, and *profits* are used interchangeably.

Accounts receivable—the amount of money owed to the firm from credit sales but not yet collected.

Inventories—raw materials, work-in-progress, and finished goods.

Fixed assets—plant, property, and equipment. Property is not assumed to lose economic value over time but all other fixed assets are. The term *gross fixed assets* refers to the purchase price of the assets. Accumulated depreciation is the sum of the depreciation of the fixed assets over prior time periods. *Net fixed assets* is gross fixed assets less accumulated depreciation.

Short-term debt—loans payable in the next year. Short-term debt may take the form of notes payable or bank loans.

Accounts payable—the amount the firm owes to suppliers for goods and services purchased on credit.

Accruals—costs that have been expensed on the *Income Statement* but are yet to be paid. These typically include rent, wages, taxes, and utilities.

Current portion of the long-term debt—principal due in the next year on long-term debt issued in the past.

Long-term debt—debt due in more than one year.

Preferred stock—a hybrid of debt and stock. More detail is included in Chapter 7.

Stockholders' equity—common stock plus retained earnings.

Assignment 1

Construct the *Income Statement* and *Balance Sheet* from the following list of items. Recall that

COGS = Beginning inventory + Materials purchased – Ending inventory

Category	2009
Accounts payable	37,000
Accounts receivable	9,000
Accruals	2,000
Accumulated depreciation	25,000
Advertising expenditures	15,000
Beginning inventory	300,000
Capital surplus	91,000
Cash	39,900
Common stock @par	30,000
Depreciation expense	30,000
Ending Inventory	73,100
Gross fixed assets	320,000
Interest expense	38,000
Lease payments	12,000
Long-term debt	156,000
Management salaries	25,000
Materials purchases	200,000
Net fixed assets	295,000
Notes payable	21,000
R&D expenditures	10,000
Repairs and maintenance costs	8,000
Retained earnings	80,000
Sales	600,000
Taxes	24,000

Assignment 2

Construct the *Common-sized Income Statement* and *Balance Sheet* using the information from Assignment 1.

Ratios

1. Liquidity Ratios

$$Current\ ratio = \frac{Current\ Assets}{Current\ Liabilities}$$

$$Quick\ ratio = \frac{Current\ Assets - Inventory}{Current\ Liabilities}$$

2. Asset Utilization Ratios

$$Avg.\ Collection\ Period = \frac{Accounts\ Receivable}{Sales/365}$$

$$Inventory\ turnover\ ratio = \frac{COGS}{Inventory}$$

$$Total\ Asset\ Turnover = \frac{Sales}{Total\ Assets}$$

$$Inventory\ Conversion\ period = \frac{Inventory}{COGS/365}$$

$$Payables\ conversion\ period = \frac{Accounts\ Payable}{COGS/365}$$

3. Debt Utilization Ratios

$$Debt\ ratio = \frac{Total\ Debt}{Total\ Assets}$$

$$Times\ interest\ earned = \frac{EBIT}{Interest\ Expense}$$

4. Profitability Ratios

$$ROA = \frac{Net\ Income}{Total\ Assets}$$

$$ROE = \frac{Net\ Income}{Equity}$$

$$Gross\ profit\ margin = \frac{Gross\ Profit}{Sales}$$

$$Operating\ profit\ margin = \frac{Operating\ Profit}{Sales}$$

$$Net\ profit\ margin = \frac{Net\ Income}{Sales}$$

5. Combination Ratios

Cash conversion cycle = inventory conversion period + average collection period – payables conversion period:

$$ROE = \left(\frac{Net\ Income}{Sales}\right) \times \left(\frac{Sales}{Assets}\right) \times \left(\frac{Assets}{Equity}\right)$$

$$Equity\ Multiplier = \frac{Total\ Assets}{Equity}$$

Assignment 3

Calculate the above ratios using the information in Assignment 1.

STUDY PACKET:
FINANCIAL STATEMENTS

Below is a set of concepts not discussed in Derek's meeting with Mr. Bensen. Nonetheless, they are important.

Equations

Net income = dividends paid + [current year's retained earnings − previous year's retained earnings]

Number of shares outstanding = common stock at par / par value

Effective rate on trade credit = $(1 + r)^n - 1$

Note: Companies often deliver goods or perform services and bill the customer. The customer is typically given a discount if they pay within a specified time frame but must pay the full amount if they pay after the discount period expires. For example, payment terms may be 2/10 net 30. This means the customer may take a 2% discount if they pay within 10 days. If they don't pay by day 10, they must pay the full amount by day 30. The customer could borrow money from a bank on day 10 and receive the discount or wait until day 30 to pay. The above equation gives the effective rate of waiting until day 30 to pay.

Example

Trade terms are 2/10 net 30. Hence, a firm may pay $98 in 10 days rather than the full $100 in 30 days. Waiting to pay on day 30 is essentially a 20 day loan from the supplier. The effective annual rate on the loan is:

$$\textit{Effective rate on trade credit} = (1+2/98)^{\left(\frac{365}{20}\right)} - 1 = 44.59\%$$

Therefore, the firm should pay at day 10 if it can borrow from other sources at an effective annual rate of less than 44.59%.

PROBLEM SET

The *Income Statement* and *Balance Sheets* below are from Chapter 4 with slight modifications to illustrate two concepts.

Income Statement 12-31-1998	
Sales	100,000
COGS	25,000
Gross profit	75,000
Operating expenses	45,000
Depreciation	3,000
Operating profit	27,000
Interest expense	1,000
EBT	26,000
Taxes	10,400
Net Income	15,600

Balance Sheet 12-31-1997

Cash	40,000	Notes payable	0
Accounts receivable	20,000	Accounts payable	2,000
Inventory	25,000	Accruals	1,000
Current Assets	85,000	Current portion LTD	0
Gross fixed assets	80,000	**Current Liabilities**	3,000
Accumulated depreciation	4,000	Long-term debt	110,000
Net fixed assets	76,000	Preferred stock	0
Total Assets	161,000	Common stock ($0.25 par)	2,500
		Additional paid in capital	44,500
		Retained earnings	1,000
		Total Liabilities & Equity	161,000

Balance Sheet 12-31-1998

Cash	33,000	Notes payable	0
Accounts receivable	22,000	Accounts payable	2,000
Inventory	35,600	Accruals	1,000
Current Assets	**90,600**	Current portion LTD	110,000
Gross fixed assets	93,000	**Current Liabilities**	**113,000**
Accumulated depreciation	7,000	Long-term debt	0
Net fixed assets	86,000	Preferred stock	0
Total Assets	**176,600**	Common stock ($0.25 par)	2,500
		Additional paid in capital	49,100
		Retained earnings	12,000
		Total Liabilities & Equity	**176,600**

Questions

Natasha made these notes for her intern to review as he learns the business.

Eric Bensen and Alex Romero want funding for Caspian Sea Drinks. They brought financial statements to my office today. They will present to the group in two weeks.

Bad news:
1. Eric and Alex don't understand financial statements. They listed a one-year loan as long-term debt. They even put it on the 12-31-1997 Balance Sheet even though the loan was made in 1998.
2. The current ratio and the quick ratio clearly show they are in danger of bankruptcy. Those boys should have seen this coming.
3. Operating expenses are going up as a percentage of Sales. They say increased advertising is the reason. This is acceptable but we must keep a close watch.

Good news:
1. Sales are growing.
2. Profit margin and ROE are strong.
3. Caspian Sea is a good product.
4. Other than the $110,000 due in a few weeks CSD has no debt.
5. They have positive cash flow from operations.
6. A cash infusion large enough to pay off the debt and buy equipment could make this a great money machine.

Bottom line:
A cash infusion will save the business. The boys are not dishonest; they just don't understand financial statements. We can fix that.

1. If you were one of the angel investors would you buy equity in Caspian Sea Drinks? Debt? What questions would you want to ask Bensen?
2. How many shares of stock are there?
3. What was the total dividend payment? The dividend payment per share?
4. A firm offers trade credit terms of 1/10 net 40. What is the effective rate of trade credit?

4.1

Derek was focused on showing Moss that he'd made an effort. He thought about how to do that in the elevator on the way down to the ground floor. Two significant things had happened: the sinister grin and Mr. Bensen getting up to leave in a hurry without a handshake. These things were significant to him and for the first time he had some reason to question Mr. Bensen's authenticity. He hadn't really made an effort, but he was closer to seeing things from Moss's perspective. He hoped that would be enough.

It wasn't. Derek and Moss met again. They walked to the bench in the park and Derek told him about the significant developments from the meeting. Moss stood up, crossed his arms, and took several steps away from the bench. He stopped, put his hands in his pockets, and walked, stiffly, back to the bench. He sat down and looked at Derek.

"How many of these meetings are you gonna have?" Moss asked.

"What do you mean?"

"How many meetings? How long are you gonna come here and get tutored by your mentor?"

"I don't know," Derek said. He realized he hadn't thought about that.

"Listen. I'm glad to hear you're finally seeing a reason to question Bensen's integrity. Trust me—start there and follow that path of mistrust and it'll lead to some pretty dark stuff. At least you're where you need to be to start getting things done. I'm just worried it's gonna take too long." Moss rubbed the length of his face with both hands. "Are you always with him when you're in the building?"

"Yeah, pretty much."

"You need a reason to wander around, take a walk down to Research and Development or something and see what you can see."

Derek nodded, "Okay. That's an idea."

"Yeah. See if you can come up with one or two more. I'll see you next week." Moss stood and kicked at a walnut before walking away, slowly, with his hands in his pockets.

—

Throughout the week, Derek thought about his situation. Mr. Bensen's face in the window was strange, but the more time passed, the less confident he was about his interpretation of the grin. *He could've been looking out the window down at the street and seen something interesting or strange. It looked like he was looking at me, but he might not've seen me at all.* On the other hand, he knew there was something in Mr. Bensen's face that made him uncomfortable.

Derek didn't know what he would do if he took a walk down to Research and Development as Moss had suggested, but he knew that if he at least figured out where it was, he could tell Moss he'd done something.

—

As Derek walked toward the building for his next meeting, he kept his eye on a girl in front of him in a black skirt and white sweater. She had shiny hair. He'd been several feet behind her for a few blocks and he'd seen several men and women take notice of her. He was surprised when she walked into the large lobby of the building that housed Caspian Sea. He kept the same quick walking pace he'd established on the street to keep up with her without overtaking her. The first few times he'd walked into the building he'd gaped around like a tourist, looking up through the glass ceiling at the rising elevators, often full of people, few of whom ever looked out at the city or down at him. But this time he was focused. Not just on the girl, but on getting something accomplished. Everyone else looked focused. He walked to the bank of elevators. So did the girl. Of the five elevators, he preferred the one in the middle. She stood in front of the one on the far end. He watched the numbers above each elevator count up and down and was disappointed that the middle one was going up. He thought it might be worth trying the one on the end this time. He still hadn't seen the girl's face.

He felt a pat on his arm. It was Mr. Bensen, who was talking on his mobile phone. Mr. Bensen smiled, pointed at his phone and made an exasperated face, held up one finger, raised his eyebrows, turned and stepped away from the elevators. Derek was suddenly distracted. He wasn't ready to think about Mr. Bensen. He was thinking about the girl. He was thinking about Research and Development. He hadn't developed a plan to get to Research and Development yet, but he'd at least been able to picture himself walking through its offices, wherever they were located in the building. But now he had something else to figure out. He stopped thinking about the girl.

He was sure that Mr. Bensen was indicating that he was stuck in an annoying phone conversation which he preferred not to bring with him on an elevator. But he wasn't sure what the one finger gesture meant. *Is he asking me to wait? Maybe he's been waiting for me and is going to surprise me with a field trip to the factory or something. Maybe Research and Development is on another floor and he's gonna take me there—or maybe it's at the factory—that would make sense.* It was 1:30 pm. Normally they met at 3:00 pm, but Mr. Bensen had emailed Derek to ask if they could move the time up. Derek didn't think much about it. *Maybe we're going out for lunch. I've heard these guys eat late sometimes. I could handle that.*

Derek had plowed through a cheese burrito an hour ago, but was still hungry. *But he would've called and told me if that was his plan. But maybe he just had the idea a few minutes before—maybe he'd been on the phone through his lunch and hadn't eaten yet—and because he couldn't call me, he came down to the lobby to catch me before I went up. Lunch out with the CEO of Caspian Sea—no cheese burritos there. But if we went somewhere nearby, we might run into Moss. He knows we're meeting early. He's probably blowing government money on expensive lunches and drinks. If we did, I bet he'd try something, like approach the table and ask for a light.*

Derek turned around. Mr. Bensen was still on the phone, facing the opposite direction, looking into the lobby. *Maybe he's just saying, "See you up there in a minute." That probably makes the most sense. But what if that's not it? What if I ride up there, he looks up and sees me on the elevator and wonders why when he's just asked me to wait? Then he's gotta come up and get me to come back down to go out for lunch? No way he'd do that. He'd just go grab a sandwich, bring it up with him, and then tell me "I was gonna take you out for a real meal, but ... "*

The bell rang and the doors of the elevator at the far end opened. Several people stepped off and even more crowded in. Mr. Bensen still had his back to Derek. Derek didn't move. The girl was one of the last to enter the elevator. He saw her face. It was a pretty face—pageant pretty—young and bright and happy. She smiled out at Derek and raised her eyebrows and nodded to him as if to say, *There's room if you're going up. I can hold the door.* Derek gulped. He raised his eyebrows and shook his head, then raised his eyebrows again, not sure what he had communicated. The young woman shrugged and the doors closed.

"What's the problem? She's cute," Mr. Bensen said over Derek's right shoulder.

"Hey. I uh ... You off the phone?"

"Yeah. My mom. Yeah, I'm pretty sure she was checking you out. You got a girlfriend?"

"No. No girlfriend. That girl? Way out of my league. Anyway, I'm no good in crowded elevators."

"If you say so," Mr. Bensen said. "Let's see if you can handle this one." The bell rang and the middle elevator's doors opened. Derek stepped on and Mr. Bensen followed. Mr. Bensen moved to the corner of the elevator and said, "I'll give you as much room as possible. You know, if these had glass on all sides, you could watch and see what floor she gets off on. Too bad."

Derek smiled and shrugged and looked out at the city as the elevator rose. He'd walked into the building with some focus, but the last two minutes had thrown him all over the place. He was relieved, at least, that he hadn't had the opportunity to misinterpret Mr. Bensen's gesture. All he did was tell a tiny white lie; He had absolutely no problem with elevators. *But what's a white lie? I'm gonna need more of those if I'm gonna take a walk down to Research and Development.*

CHAPTER 5

THE STATEMENT OF CASH FLOWS:
THE LIFEBLOOD OF A CORPORATION

They stepped off the elevator and walked by Mrs. Howe's desk and toward the conference room.

"So, I had an awkward lunch today," Mr. Bensen said. "Funny timing considering what we're talking about today. A business acquaintance told me he wanted to *pick my brain*. Turns out he wanted to pick my pocket—wanted a massive bail out. He's bleeding cash. You'll hear analysts say that about companies. They're *bleeding cash* or *hemorrhaging cash* or they'll say a company needs a *cash infusion*. That's how important cash is. It's the lifeblood of a corporation. Without blood, humans die. Without money, a corporation dies. A corporation can have a great product, great employees, and do everything right, but if it runs out of money, it's finished." Mr. Bensen opened the door of the conference room for Derek and they walked in and sat.

"Today we're talking about blood flow—cash flow. If you go to the Caspian Sea Drinks exhibit at the Coke Museum you'll see how Caspian Sea is made, bottled, and delivered. Most people see workers, equipment, and trucks. I see the blood flowing—the cash flowing. Workers have to be paid, supplies have to be bought, trucks have to be filled with diesel. Everything Caspian Sea Drinks does requires money. Manage it right and everybody is happy. Make a mistake and you could be bankrupt.

"When we started Caspian Sea Drinks we had no idea what a *Statement of Cash Flow* was. We thought if we had a good product, we could sell it and everything would be fine. If it hadn't been for Natasha and the angel investors we wouldn't have made it. It turns out there are three types of cash flow—*Cash Flow from Operations*, *Cash Flow from Investing*, and *Cash Flow from Financing*. Look at Caspian Sea's old *Income Statement* and *Balance Sheet* and I'll walk you through constructing a *Statement of Cash Flows* and what Natasha was looking for."

Derek flipped through his folder and found and pulled out the following statements:

Income Statement 12-31-1998	
Sales	100,000
COGS	25,000
Gross profit	75,000
Operating expenses	45,000
Depreciation	3,000
Operating profit	27,000
Interest expense	1,000
EBT	26,000
Taxes	10,400
Net Income	15,600

Balance Sheet 12-31-1997

Cash	40,000	Notes payable	0
Accounts receivable	20,000	Accounts payable	2,000
Inventory	25,000	Accruals	1,000
Current Assets	**85,000**	Current portion LTD	0
Gross fixed assets	80,000	**Current Liabilities**	**3,000**
Accumulated depreciation	4,000	Long-term debt	110,000
Net fixed assets	76,000	Preferred stock	0
Total Assets	**161,000**	Common stock	47,000
		Retained earnings	1,000
		Total Liabilities & Equity	**161,000**

Balance Sheet 12-31-1998

Cash	33,000	Notes payable	0
Accounts receivable	22,000	Accounts payable	2,000
Inventory	35,600	Accruals	1,000
Current Assets	**90,600**	Current portion LTD	110,000
Gross fixed assets	93,000	**Current Liabilities**	**113,000**
Accumulated depreciation	7,000	Long-term debt	0
Net fixed assets	86,000	Preferred stock	0
Total Assets	**176,600**	Common stock	47,000
		Retained earnings	16,600
		Total Liabilities & Equity	**176,600**

"Let's start with the easy calculation, *Total Cash Flow*. At the end of 1997, we had $40,000. At the end of 1998 we had $33,000. We burned through $7,000 in cash. That's not necessarily good or bad. If we had burned through all of it, that would be bad—no money, no blood, death, bankruptcy. But it's not necessarily bad news that we had less cash at the end of 1998 than at the end of 1997. Maybe we were doing really great things with the cash. Natasha wanted to know what was going on. She started by looking at *Cash Flow from Operations*.

"We want *Cash Flow from Operations* to be positive. Again, think of a corporation as a money machine. We put money in one side of the machine and hope to get more out of the other side. *Cash Flow from Operations* tells us if we are, in fact, making more money. Operations is what we do. Maybe it's not making money now. Maybe it'll take some time to get the machine up to speed, but eventually—hopefully soon—this has got to be a positive number.

"*Cash Flow from Operations* is all about the *Income Statement*," Mr. Bensen said. "Here's how you calculate it." He stood up and wrote on the board.

Net income	15,600
Depreciation	+ 3,000
Change in Accounts Receivable	-2,000
Change in Inventory	-10,600
Change in Accounts Payable	0
Change in Accruals	0
Total CF from Operations	6,000

"Hold on," Derek said. "I'm confused. You have *Balance Sheet* stuff up there. You said it was all about the *Income Statement*."

Mr. Bensen sat down and talked while Derek looked at the board. "We're trying to see how much cash we actually collected for the year as a result of our operations—as a result of making and selling Caspian Sea. We start with net income. But that's not an amount of cash we actually collected. We have to make some adjustments based on accounting rules.

"We add *Depreciation*. *Depreciation* is not a cash flow, but we subtracted it from our gross profit for tax purposes. *Accounts Receivable* went up. Subtract. *Accounts Receivable* means we sold stuff but were promised we'd be paid later instead of being paid up front. Those transactions show up in the *Sales* entry on the *Income Statement* even though we didn't collect any money. Our *Accounts Receivable* went up. That means the *Sales* number overstated the amount of cash we collected. By subtracting the increase in *Accounts Receivable*, we adjust net income to reflect cash collected. You would add the difference if *Accounts Receivable* went down.

"*Inventory* went up too," Mr. Bensen said. "Subtract. Here's an easy way to think of it: we have more bottles of Caspian Sea to sell, it cost us money to get those bottles, so subtract. Doing this adjusts *COGS* for actual money spent purchasing material. You would add the difference if inventory went down. *Accounts Payable* and accruals didn't change. Do nothing. If it had increased, then you'd add the difference. If it had decreased, you'd subtract. Do the opposite of *Accounts Receivable*. This adjusts operating expenses for actual cash flows. Make sense?"

"I think so," Derek said.

"Natasha looked at all this and saw we were doing something right. We were making money selling the product. Our problem was elsewhere. She looked at *Cash Flow from Investing*. *Cash Flow from Investing* has two components but we're just concerned with one—buying or selling equipment. This is easy. It's just the change in *gross fixed assets*. In this case *gross fixed assets* increased by $13,000. That means we bought plant, property, or equipment. Subtract. If it were a decrease, you'd add. So, total *Cash Flow from Investing*—$13,000.

"A negative cash flow for investing is probably good and a positive one is probably bad," said Mr. Bensen. "We needed to buy more equipment because we needed to make more Caspian Sea because people were buying it as fast as we could make it. Natasha saw this and knew that we were using money to grow. If *Cash Flow from Investing* had been positive, then we must have been selling off equipment. That's not a sign of a growing business. Again, a negative *Cash Flow from Investing* was good. It meant we were buying equipment and growing." Mr. Bensen stopped and looked at Derek.

It took him a second to realize that Mr. Bensen was checking to make sure that he was following. "Yeah. Okay. I'm with you."

"Okay. Finally, *Cash Flow from Financing.* Financing is the source of our money. This is the money we put into the machine. It is then used to buy *Fixed Assets (Cash Flow from Investing)* or used in *Operations (Cash Flow from Operations).* Positive or negative *Cash Flow from Financing* could be good news or bad news or neither. Here's how it's calculated." Mr. Bensen got up and wrote on the board.

Change in notes payable	0
Change in current portion of long-term debt	110,000
Change in long-term debt	-110,000
Change in common stock	0
Dividends paid	0
Total cash flow from financing	0

"Borrowing money or selling stock is a *positive* cash flow. Repaying debt or buying back stock or paying dividends is a *negative* cash flow. We were doing none of the above. The only thing that changed was that our long-term debt was becoming short-term debt because it was about to mature. Here. Add all three cash flows together and you get the total cash flow." Mr. Bensen wrote on the board again.

CF operations	6,000
CF investing	-13,000
CF financing	0
Total CF	-7,000

"Now Natasha could see our problem. Suppose the next year we had the same success in selling Caspian Sea. Our *Cash Flow from Operations* would be the same. Suppose we did not buy any new equipment. Then our cash flows would be ... " Mr. Bensen wrote on the board again.

CF operations	6,000
CF investing	0
CF financing	-110,000
Total CF	-104,000

"The debt was coming due and we would have to pay it. If we didn't pay, we'd be bankrupt. Back then Caspian Sea Drinks was a small company so this is a simple example. Natasha could see our problem before constructing a *Statement of Cash Flow*. However, the principle applies to large, complex firms. You have to have blood. As humans, we don't think too much about where the blood comes from and where it goes. Doctors are paid well to know all that for us. If you're in Finance, you're a doctor. As a CEO, I'm my own doctor. I need to know if I'm bleeding. If I am, I need to know how to stop it. As an investor, I need to be able to diagnose. I can't invest in a firm that is about to bleed out."

"Heartless," said Derek and grinned.

"Bloodless," said Mr. Bensen and stood up. "That's it for this week. Sorry it was a bit rushed and a bit gory."

"No problem," Derek said.

"Let's walk down to the office—I left the Study Packet stuff in there." They stood and walked out of the room.

PROBLEM SET

Eric and Alex met with venture capitalists in New York in order to convince them to invest in Caspian Sea. Unbeknownst to them, the VCs are considering three companies that weekend. The following are the *Income Statement* and *Balance Sheet* for the three companies that are identified only as companies A, B, and C. Construct a *Common-sized Balance Sheet* and *Income Statement*, the ratios of the Study Packet in Chapter 4, and a *Statement of Cash Flows* for each firm. In which company should the VCs invest? Notice if the given numbers are in millions or thousands.

Company A (all numbers in millions)

Income Statement (prior year)		Balance Sheet (prior year)			
		Assets		Liabilities & Equity	
Sales	35,119	Cash	11,337	Notes payable	4,376
COGS	12,693	Accounts rec	6,011	Accounts payable	8,132
Gross profit	22,426	Inventories	4,231	Accruals	1,000
Operating exp.	13,977	**Current Assets**	**21,579**	Current portion LTD	5,000
Depreciation	2,500	Net fixed assets	51,342	**Current Liabilities**	**18,508**
EBIT	5,949	**Total Assets**	**72,921**	Long-term debt	14,041
Interest exp	733			Common stock	10,937
EBT	5,216			Retained earnings	29,435
Taxes	2,085			**Total Liabilities & Equity**	**72,921**
Net Income	3,131				

Income Statement (current year)		Balance Sheet (current year)			
		Assets		Liabilities & Equity	
Sales	46,542	Cash	14,035	Notes payable	9,912
COGS	18,216	Accounts rec	6,645	Accounts payable	7,871
Gross profit	28,326	Inventories	4,817	Accruals	1,500
Operating exp.	18,172	**Current Assets**	**25,497**	Current portion LTD	5,000
Depreciation	2,800	Net fixed assets	54,477	**Current Liabilities**	**24,283**
EBIT	7,354	**Total Assets**	**79,974**	Long-term debt	13,656
Interest exp	417			Common stock	12,092
EBT	6,937			Retained earnings	29,943
Taxes	2,775			**Total Liabilities & Equity**	**79,974**
Net Income	4,162				

Company B (all numbers in millions)

Income Statement (prior year)		Balance Sheet (prior year)			
		Assets		**Liabilities & Equity**	
Sales	4,636	Cash	315	Notes payable	404
COGS	2,234	Accounts rec	689	Accounts payable	316
Gross profit	2,402	Inventories	305	Accruals	568
Operating exp.	1,995	**Current Assets**	**1,309**	Current portion LTD	50
Depreciation	100	Net fixed assets	7,550	**Current Liabilities**	**1,338**
EBIT	307	**Total Assets**	**8,859**	Long-term debt	1,687
Interest exp	128			Common stock	2,285
EBT	179			Retained earnings	3,549
Taxes	70			**Total Liabilities & Equity**	**8,859**
Net Income	109				

Income Statement (current year)		Balance Sheet (current year)			
		Assets		**Liabilities & Equity**	
Sales	4,500	Cash	300	Notes payable	652
COGS	2,250	Accounts rec	900	Accounts payable	595
Gross profit	2,250	Inventories	669	Accruals	618
Operating exp.	2,000	**Current Assets**	**1,869**	Current portion LTD	50
Depreciation	100	Net fixed assets	7,414	**Current Liabilities**	**1,915**
EBIT	150	**Total Assets**	**9,283**	Long-term debt	2,256
Interest exp	114			Common stock	1,633
EBT	36			Retained earnings	3,479
Taxes	9			**Total Liabilities & Equity**	**9,283**
Net Income	27				

Company C (all numbers in thousands)

Income Statement (prior year)		Balance Sheet (prior year)			
		Assets		Liabilities & Equity	
Sales	150,000	Cash	60,000	Notes payable	0
COGS	65,000	Accounts rec	19,600	Accounts payable	18,400
Gross profit	85,000	Inventories	16,700	Accruals	1,000
Operating exp.	30,000	**Current Assets**	**96,300**	Current portion LTD	0
Depreciation	1,800	Net fixed assets	38,400	**Current Liabilities**	**19,400**
EBIT	53,200	**Total Assets**	**134,700**	Long-term debt	0
Interest exp	0			Common stock	80,000
EBT	53,200			Retained earnings	35,300
Taxes	21,000			**Total Liabilities & Equity**	**134,700**
Net Income	32,200				

Income Statement (current year)		Balance Sheet (current year)			
		Assets		Liabilities & Equity	
Sales	180,000	Cash	77,000	Notes payable	0
COGS	72,500	Accounts rec	30,000	Accounts payable	17,600
Gross profit	107,500	Inventories	20,000	Accruals	1,100
Operating exp.	34,000	**Current Assets**	**127,000**	Current portion LTD	0
Depreciation	2,000	Net fixed assets	50,500	**Current Liabilities**	**18,700**
EBIT	71,500	**Total Assets**	**177,500**	Long-term debt	0
Interest exp	0			Common stock	80,000
EBT	71,500			Retained earnings	78,800
Taxes	28,000			**Total Liabilities & Equity**	**177,500**
Net Income	43,500				

5.1

Derek stopped just outside the conference room door, swallowed, cleared his throat, and asked, "What's down this way?"

"What or *who*?"

"Huh?" Derek asked.

"I was gonna tell you as you were leaving—give you something to think about—looks like you've already been thinking."

Derek was confused. *What did I ask him? I thought I just asked him what was down the hall.*

"She works for us," Mr. Bensen said. "The girl from the elevator. She's down there somewhere—Marketing? Research and Development?—I'm not sure."

Derek stood still. He felt the blood in his face. He hadn't forgotten about Research and Development, but he had forgotten about the girl. He couldn't believe they could be connected.

"You're on your own there, buddy," Mr. Bensen said. "But feel free to take a walk and do some recon work if you feel so led. First, come down and pick up your Study Packet."

Derek followed Mr. Bensen to his office, took the Study Packet, and walked toward the elevator.

"Not up for the challenge just yet?" Mr. Bensen asked. "That's cool. I'd be the same way. No pressure from here. See you next week."

"Next week," Derek said, forced a grin, and walked toward the elevator. On the way down, Derek felt an overwhelming sense of relief. *Finally! Something is happening. I've got something to tell Moss. He's gotta count this as some kind of progress. He said Marketing or Research and Development. I just tell Moss she's in Research and Development. Nothing wrong with that.*

Outside, Derek didn't see Moss waiting for him as usual. Derek had told him he was meeting Mr. Bensen earlier than usual and Moss told him he could be there at 2:30 pm. It was 2:35 pm. Walking away from the building, Derek sent Moss a text message telling him he had something to report and that he'd meet him in the park. Before Derek got to the street, a reply came back: "About time. I'm here."

Moss didn't get up when Derek walked toward the bench and sat. "Let's hear it," he said.

"There's a girl who works in Research and Development. She's pretty hot. She's sort of into me." Derek realized how flimsy the whole thing was as he heard himself say it.

"Now we're talking. Good. So what's your plan?"

"I don't know. I mean, I'm gonna talk to her—I've got to. I sort of just found out, so I'm not sure. But I will talk to her. I'll know more next week."

"Relax. Here's what you do," Moss said. "A cup of coffee. Next week. She probably gets off at 5:00. You just go across the street when you're done and wait for her—piece of cake." Moss stood up and grinned. Derek stood and didn't say anything. They shook hands. "Hero, buddy. You're on your way. You'll find that the heroic road often comes with these kinds of benefits." He winked at Derek and walked away.

—

Derek had visualized heads turning as he held the door open for the girl with the shiny hair as she walked into the coffee shop in her skirt and sweater. He'd squint around the room with confidence, looking for a place for them to sit. Then he'd point her in the direction of a free table and ask what she wanted to drink. He'd order and bring the drinks to her. She'd smile at him as he approached, the way she smiled at him from inside the elevator. He'd sit and they'd talk, and he'd very discreetly inch closer to asking if she knew about the ingredients of Caspian Sea.

He'd visualized it, but when he got to the building and looked across the street at the real coffee shop, he realized all the things that would have to happen before he opened that door for the girl. He was struck with fear. He was beyond distracted. He was terrified that he'd see the girl in the lobby or on the elevator or that she'd be standing at Mrs. Howe's desk when he walked in the office.

He made his way up to Mr. Bensen's floor. No girl anywhere. Mrs. Howe was on the phone. Derek waved at her as he walked toward the conference room. He could see the door was open. He took a deep breath as he walked. He'd done his homework. He knew his stuff. He was a student and that's all he could be for the next hour.

"How ya doin'?" Mr. Bensen asked from his chair as Derek walked into the conference room.

"Good. You?" Derek replied and put his things on the table.

"Good," Mr. Bensen said, and nodded.

CHAPTER 6

BONDS:
FEEDING THE CORPORATE MONEY MACHINE I

S o," Mr. Bensen began. "You remember the story. When Alex and I first formed Caspian Sea Drinks, LLC, we needed money. We used my credit card and the money we had but that wasn't enough. Spencer bought 30% of the company for $40,000. Stovall loaned Caspian Sea $100,000. Remember, Alex and I didn't get that money. Caspian Sea Drinks, LLC got it and used it to buy the equipment and supplies we needed to make enough Caspian Sea to meet the growing demand. That's what small companies do. That's what big companies like Coke do. To raise money to fund growth, a firm will sell equity or debt. Today we're gonna talk about debt. Next week we'll talk about equity.

"When Stovall loaned Caspian Sea $100,000 none of us really knew what we were doing. None of us knew what a bond was, but we still managed to issue one."

"What do you mean?" Derek asked.

"Well, technically it wasn't a bond, but effectively it was. We promised to pay Stovall a certain amount on a certain date. If we didn't make the payment then he took control of the company. In return he wrote a check to Caspian Sea. That's how bonds work.

"Here's a question. If a friend asks to borrow $100, what's your first question? What makes you decide to say *yes* or *no*?"

Without thinking Derek said, "Normally I don't have any money, but … " he caught himself. "I mean, that's what I tell people. *I don't have any money.*"

"Okay. But let's say you do."

"Okay. Well, it really depends on who's asking," Derek said. "I've got some *friends* who I know would never pay me back. I'd never loan them money. There are other friends who would only ask if they really needed it and I'd give them the money without thinking about whether or not they'd pay me back."

"Someone you're not sure about," Mr. Bensen said. "Someone who's not an idiot, but you wouldn't necessarily die for."

"Yeah, there are a few folks I wouldn't be sure about. I guess I'd ask, *Why do you need it?* and *When will you pay me back?*"

"Okay. It's the same with companies. Except there are no companies I'd give money to without thinking about getting it back—just because I like them. Maybe Chick-fil-A—I'd hate to see them go out of business."

"Can't imagine the world without Chick-fil-A," Derek said. For a second he visualized taking the girl out for a milkshake instead of a coffee. Then he scolded himself for losing focus.

"Okay. Let's not get all emotional," Mr. Bensen sat up and cleared his throat. "Back to Finance. All companies have a credit rating. The higher the rating, the more you can trust them. Just like with your friends. But with companies, analysts from Standard & Poor's, Moody's, and/or Fitch pore over the financials of the company and give each one an exact grade. Then potential bond buyers like Stovall can know how trustworthy—the technical term is *creditworthy*—a company is. Even then the first question sophisticated investors ask is, *What are you going to do with the money?* The same as you asking *Why do you need it?* Why do you ask that?"

"Depends," Derek said. "Some people aren't all that responsible. I had a guy last year begging me for money for lottery tickets when the jackpot was high. He was afraid a winner would be drawn before he could buy all the tickets he wanted. Said he'd pay me back when he got paid the next week."

"And?" Mr. Bensen asked.

"I didn't give him anything."

"It's the same with companies," Mr. Bensen said. Some have plans to do dumb things with the money. Some have plans to do really creative and brilliant things. Every bond issue has a contract that tells potential buyers exactly how much and when they will get paid. It also tells them what the firm will and will not do with the money.

"Bonds are not just issued by corporations. There are municipal bonds—everybody calls them *munis*. They are issued by states and local governments to do things like build roads, public transportation, schools, and hospitals. The U.S. government and other countries issue bonds, too.

"Here's an example," Mr. Bensen turned over a piece of paper and drew on the back. "Assume today is June 1, 2012. Bonds used to be physical certificates like this. They were called *bearer bonds* because whoever had possession of the bond owned it. Now ownership is electronically recorded. But it's still best to think in terms of a bearer bond so you can better understand what is going on. Take a look."

Mr. Bensen turned the paper so Derek could read it.

CASPIAN SEA DRINKS BOND	
Par value = $1,000	
Coupon rate = 8.000%	
Pays semi-annually	
Matures June 1, 2015	
First interest paid on December 1, 2012	
December 1, 2014 Pay $40	June 1, 2015 Pay $40
December 1, 2013 Pay $40	June 1, 2014 Pay $40
December 1, 2012 Pay $40	June 1, 2013 Pay $40

"All bonds have a par value," he explained. "This is the amount the issuer will pay the bondholder on the maturity date. In this case, the issuer will pay $1,000 on June 1, 2015. This bond has a coupon rate of 8.000% and pays semi-annually. This means the issuer will pay the bondholder 0.08000*1,000 = $80 each year, but it will make two payments per year. The issuer will pay the bondholder $40 every six months until maturity. These payments are called coupon payments because the bondholder would physically clip the coupon and bring it to a specified bank in order to receive the payment.

"To the potential buyer, this bond is a money machine." Mr. Bensen continued. "As a rule it promises specific sizes and times of the cash flows. The investor evaluates the risk of the issuer not keeping the promise, and decides what this money machine (*the bond*) is worth. The value of any money machine (*financial asset*), regardless of whether it is called a bond or a stock or something else, is the present value of the expected future cash flows. Repeat after me. The value of any financial asset is the present value of the expected future cash flows."

Derek didn't say anything. Mr. Bensen looked at him. "Oh," Derek said, "You're serious. Sorry. Say it again."

Mr. Bensen shook his head and said, "The value of any financial asset is the present value of the expected future cash flows."

Derek parroted Mr. Bensen, "The value of any financial asset is the present value of the expected future cash flows."

"So for this bond we have the payout rule. Now we find the value by discounting the future cash flows."

Mr. Bensen wrote on the board.

$$P_0 = \frac{40}{(1+k)^1} + \frac{40}{(1+k)^2} + \frac{40}{(1+k)^3}$$
$$+ \frac{40}{(1+k)^4} + \frac{40}{(1+k)^5} + \frac{40+1{,}000}{(1+k)^6}$$

"What's k?" Derek asked. "I know it's the discount rate, but how do I know what the actual number is and why do you call it k and not r like you did when we were finding the present value of annuities? By the way this looks a lot like an annuity."

"I wrote k because that's what everybody else does. k stands for *cost of debt*. The precise number depends on the potential buyer. If you have a high credit score then you can borrow money at a relatively low rate to buy a car. If you have a low credit score then you have to pay a higher interest rate on the car loan. Some folks can't even get a loan because of their credit rating. It's the same for a corporation. The higher the score the rating agencies give the firm, the lower the interest rate, k, you will need.

"Assume k = 4.20%," Mr. Bensen said. "Then the price of the bond is $989.58. The coupon rate never changes. Visualize the old bearer bonds. If you own one, then the coupon payment is written in ink. It does not magically change. The discount rate changes. Investors looked at this bond, considered the risk, compared it to other similar bonds issued by other companies or municipalities, or the U.S. government. They decided k should be 4.20%. New information could change their mind. Let's work through a bond problem together." Mr. Bensen wrote on the board.

1. *A bond with a par value of $1,000 will mature in 4 years and make semi-annual payments. The first payment will be exactly 6 months from today. The coupon rate is 5.000%. The discount rate is 5.200%. What is the price of the bond?*

"First I need to know when the cash flows occur and how much they are," Derek said. "The coupon payment is $1,000*0.0500/2 = $25."

"Why did you divide by 2?"

"The payments are semi-annual," Derek answered "The discount rate is 5.200% but that's in annual terms so I need to use 0.0520/2 = 0.0260 in the calculation."

"Why?" Mr. Bensen asked again.

"You always quote interest rates in annual terms. Since the cash flows are semi-annual I divide by 2. So now I have," Derek wrote on the board.

$$P_0 = \frac{25}{(1.0260)^1} + \frac{25}{(1.0260)^2} + \frac{25}{(1.0260)^3} + \frac{25}{(1.0260)^4} + \frac{25}{(1.0260)^5}$$
$$+ \frac{25}{(1.0260)^6} + \frac{25}{(1.0260)^7} + \frac{25 + 1,000}{(1.0260)^8} = 992.86$$

"Perfect," Mr. Bensen said. "Financial calculators were built specifically for problems like this. On the calculator n = 8 because there are 8 payments, pmt = 25; FV = 1,000; I/y = 2.60 and solve for PV.

"Almost all bonds pay semi-annually. Almost all corporate bonds have a $1,000 par value and almost all muni bonds have a $5,000 par value. Issuers can set any payment terms they want so I cannot say that *all* corporate or *all* munis do anything. I can only say *almost all.* The important thing to remember is that they set the payout terms before they sell the bond and cannot change them after the sale.

"Okay? That's it. All this making sense?" Mr. Bensen asked. "It seems to be from the stuff you're bringing in every week."

"Yeah, it is," Derek said. "It helps to have time to process it."

"Okay. Here's your Study Packet for the week. Have fun."

STUDY PACKET: BONDS

Bonds may have fixed coupon rates or floating coupon rates. This discussion of floating rate bonds is beyond the scope of this text.

Bonds with a market price above par are said to trade at a premium while bonds with a market price below par are said to trade at a discount.

Types of Bonds by Issuer

U.S. Treasury

All Treasury issues are considered to be risk-free. They are sold in $100 par increments. They are issued through an auction process. Details of the auction may be found on the website *ustreas.gov*. The U.S. Treasury may change the types of securities it issues at any time. Below is a brief description of what is traditionally offered.

1. Treasury Bills, often referred to as T-bills, do not pay a coupon and, therefore, are called discount instruments. They are issued weekly and have a maturity of four weeks to 52 weeks.
2. Treasury Notes pay a coupon semi-annually and have a maturity from one year to ten years.

3. Treasury Bonds are identical to Treasury Notes except their maturity is more than ten years. Typically, the Treasury issues 30-year bonds.
4. TIPS or Treasury Inflation Protection Securities. Unlike T-Notes and T-Bonds, the coupon payment on TIPS changes. The coupon payment increases with inflation.
5. STRIPS stands for Separate Trading of Registered Interest and Principal of Securities. These securities are the result of a dealer buying a Treasury Note or Bond and selling the individual coupon payments to different investors.

Corporate

All types of corporations issue bonds. The majority are issued by firms in the financial sector. Almost all are $1,000 par with semi-annual coupon payments.

Municipal

Muni bonds are issued by state and local governments. Almost all are $5,000 par with semi-annual coupon payments. Most are exempt from federal income tax and state tax depending on the residence of the bond buyer. A common misconception is that all muni bonds are tax exempt. A wise investor will verify the tax status of the bonds before purchasing.

The tax exemption makes the bonds more attractive to investors, particularly those in high marginal tax brackets. An investor will be indifferent between a taxable and nontaxable bond of equal risk when the following equation holds:

$$r_m = r_t(1 - t)$$

where r_m is the yield on the municipal bond, r_t is the yield on the taxable bond, and t is the investor's marginal tax rate.

Bond Ratings and Risk Premiums

Standard & Poor's, Moody's, and Fitch all use slightly different terminology but the intent is the same. An investor will assign a default premium above the U.S. Treasury yield on an otherwise similar bond based on its rating. The following table gives a generic ratings scale:

Grade	Rating
Investment	AAA
	AA
	A
	BBB
Speculative	B
Extremely Speculative	C
In Default	D

For example, suppose a bond has a BBB rating and that investors demand a 2.50% premium for the risk associated with it. The yield on a similar Treasury is 2.00%. The investor's required rate of return on this bond is 2.00% plus 2.50% or 4.50%.

Equation

(6.1)
$$P_0 = pmt * \left[\frac{1 - \frac{1}{(1+y)^n}}{y} \right] + \frac{Par}{(1+y)^n}$$

Notice that this is exactly the same as equation 3.2 but with the last term added. P_0 is the price of the bond.

Bond issuers, like Caspian Sea Drinks, determine the payout rule for the bond. For example, CSD offers to sell a bond that has a par value of $1,000, 10 years to maturity, pays semi-annually, and has a coupon rate of 8.000%. Once CSD sets the terms, then potential investors know that the payout rule is:

$$n = 10 * 2 = 20$$
$$pmt = \$1,000 * .08/2 = \$40$$
$$FV = \$1,000$$

The investors require a certain return just like banks require a certain interest rate on a mortgage. The return investors require for loaning money to a firm (buying its bond) is called the yield-to-maturity (YTM). Suppose the required YTM is 8.20%. Then,

$$I/y = 8.20/2 = 4.10.$$

The price of the bond is then $986.53. Notice that YTM was stated in annual terms. The 'y' term in equation 6.1 is the YTM divided by 2. It is divided by 2 because the bond pays semi-annually.

If the price of the bond is known then the YTM is found by entering the payout rule and

$$PV = -986.53, [1]$$

and then solving for I/y. Finally, double I/y to find the YTM. This YTM is called the bond equivalent yield. It is not the same yield that would result from equation 3.5. The effective annual rate (also called the effective annual yield) on the bond is:

---

1   One may enter the price of the bond as a negative and future payments as a positive or vice versa.

$$EAR= (1.041)^2 - 1=0.08368$$

Knowing what bond traders mean when they quote yields in crucial. Other ways may be equally logical but will result in an incorrect price.

STRIPS example

Find the price of a $1,000 par, 20-year STRIPS with a 6.000% YTM. Then find its effective annual rate. Because STRIPS make no payments it is not clear if one should assume n to equal 20 years or 40 six-month periods. Likewise, YTM could be 6.000% or 3.000%. By market convention YTM is stated annually but calculations are done on a semi-annual basis. So,

$$n = 40$$
$$pmt = 0$$
$$FV = \$1,000$$
$$I/y = 3.000$$

The price is then $306.56.

The effective annual rate is 1.032-1 = 0.0609 or 6.09%. Now value the STRIPS with n=20 and I/y = 6.09.

There is no closed-form solution for YTM in equation 6.1. The only way to find YTM is to guess repeatedly until you find the answer or let the calculator guess for you. The calculator will be faster.

PROBLEM SET

All bonds have a par value of $1,000 unless otherwise noted.

1. Caspian Sea plans to issue a 10-year, semi-annual pay bond which has a coupon rate of 5.00%. Draw a timeline showing the payments.
2. If the YTM for the bond in #1 is 4.90%, what will the price of the bond be? Remember coupon rates and yields are stated in annual terms and this is a semi-annual pay bond.
3. Repeat # 2 assuming the YTM is 5.10%. Before doing the calculation do you think the price will increase or decrease?
4. Repeat #2 with the YTM equal to 5.00%. What do you notice about the price of the bond? This relationship will be true for any bond.
5. Caspian Sea needs to raise $15 million by issuing bonds. It plans to issue a 15-year semi-annual pay bond which has a coupon rate of 6.00%. The YTM on the bond is expected to be 6.15%. How many bonds must Caspian Sea issue? (Note: Your answer may not be a whole number. In reality, a company would not issue part of a bond.)
6. The market price of a semi-annual pay bond is $990.45. It has 20 years to maturity and a YTM of 7.090%. What is the coupon rate?
7. The market price of a semi-annual pay bond is $985.23. It has 20 years to maturity and a coupon rate of 8.00%. What is the YTM? What is the effective annual yield?
8. The market price of a semi-annual pay bond is $975.00. It has a coupon rate of 8.00% and a YTM of 8.30%. How many years are left to maturity?
9. The YTM for a 10 year STRIPS is 5.00%. It should sell for $_____.

10. The market price of a 20-year STRIPS is $306.56. The YTM is
    ____%.
11. A tax exempt muni bond has a YTM of 5.00% and an otherwise
    identical taxable corporate bond has a YTM of 8.00%. Which
    bond would an investor who has a marginal tax rate of 40%
    prefer?
12. A tax exempt muni bond with a coupon rate of 4.00% has a
    market price of 99% of par. A taxable bond with a coupon rate
    of 6.00% has a market price of 99% of par. Both bonds mature
    in 8 years and pay semi-annually. Which bond would an investor
    with a 40% marginal tax rate prefer?
13. Repeat #13 for an investor with a 30% marginal tax rate, Then
    for an investor with a 20% marginal tax rate. What type of
    investors do you think buy muni bonds?
14. The 10-year Treasury Note has a YTM of 3.00%. The table
    below shows the default risk premiums demanded by the market
    for companies with various credit ratings. Suppose a company
    with each credit rating needs to raise $20 million in debt and
    that each company plans to issue a 10-year, semi-annual pay
    bond with a coupon rate of 4.00%. How many bonds will each
    company have to sell? What are the total payments each com-
    pany must make every six months for the next 10 years? What
    is the final payment each must make?

Rating	Premium
AAA	1.00%
AA	1.50
A	1.90
BBB	2.20
BB	2.90

6.1

Derek was glad Mr. Bensen hadn't asked him about the girl. He picked up his folder and went into the bathroom, mostly so Mr. Bensen wouldn't see him walking down the hall looking for the girl or Research and Development or both, or neither.

Derek rinsed his face and leaned into the mirror. *Piece of cake. I've gotta trust Moss I guess. He didn't second guess me a bit. Mr. Bensen didn't second guess me either—my chances anyway. He's the one who said she was checking me out. Maybe I have a shot. This is what people do. This is what adults do. Adults talk to each other, sometimes over a cup of coffee. I'm not asking her to Homecoming where there's pictures and the whole town and the whole school knows. No one here cares. It's not a big deal. Don't make it a big deal.*

Derek dried his face with a couple of paper towels, made sure he looked decent and that everything was where it was supposed to be, picked up his folder, and walked out of the bathroom and took a left down the hall into unknown territory. The hallway opened up into a large room full of cubicles with offices on the outer edges. It was relatively quiet, except for the typical office sounds of clicks, beeps, and the rustling of papers. Derek had no idea where he was going, he only knew who he was looking for. *I'm okay as long as I keep walking. If I stop, someone'll ask me what I'm looking for. I can't say 'the hot girl with the white sweater.' I've just gotta walk around and get lucky.* A few people looked up or over at Derek as he walked by, but most kept working and didn't notice him. There didn't appear to be any division of offices or departments that he could tell. There wasn't a sign hanging over one section that said *Marketing* and another that said *Research and Development* or *Accounts*.

Derek scanned the faces and backs of heads and shoulders he could see—nothing, no one, looked familiar. In about 30 feet or so, the large room ended and another hallway led to what he assumed was another large room on the other side. She walked out of that hallway. She looked right at him and smiled. She was wearing dark grey pants with a white blouse—looked just as nice as she had two weeks before—nicer. *Stunning. What now? She smiled. Again. What does that mean?* Derek returned the smile. He didn't know how he kept walking. They each took six or seven steps and stopped in front of each other. "I know you," she said.

"Derek," Derek said and stuck out his hand.

"Molly," the girl said. She moved a few folders from one hand to the other and shook his hand gently, mostly with her fingers. "I *thought* you worked here. I offered you an elevator ride."

She's flirting, isn't she? This is unbelievable! A woman walked by and Derek thought he saw her shake her head and grin. "Yeah. I, uh, I was waiting for Mr. Bensen."

"And where are you headed now?"

This is too easy. "Actually, I was looking around," Derek fumbled and put his hands in his pockets, then took one out to rub his eye for no reason. "Well, I was looking for you."

"I don't believe that," Molly said, clutching the folders to her chest like a schoolgirl.

"Yes you do," Derek said, suddenly confident, and also aware that other people could hear them talking. A few more had glanced over and then looked away with the same grin as the woman who'd walked by earlier. "How about we meet for a cup of coffee?"

"Okay," she said.

"What time are you done here?"

"5:00 sharp," Molly grinned.

"Okay. 5:00. Just across the street. I'll make sure there's a table."

"Great. See ya soon." They didn't shake hands again and each headed off in the same direction as before. Derek had no idea where he was going. He walked down the hallway, then into and along the length of the other large room. He came to another hallway that led to a stairwell. He didn't want to risk walking back through the office and running into Molly again. *Seriously, she could be in magazines! And she's flirting with me! But the way everyone was grinning. There's something going on there.* Derek walked into the stairwell and went down a flight of stairs. He figured he could walk through the office below and find the elevator without trouble. The door was locked. He went down another flight and that door was locked too. He continued down the stairs. He stopped trying doors on the 14th floor. He had to sit down twice, at the 14th and the 6th floor, not because he was tired, but because he was dizzy.

By the time he got to the coffee shop and sat down at a table, it was 4:47 pm. He sat back and took a breath, still a bit dizzy and very confused about what had happened in the last hour. *What was the deal with all the grins and head shakes in the office? This girl must flirt with everyone. That's the only thing that would make sense. No way she has a boyfriend. Maybe she does have a boyfriend and that's why people were shaking their heads. But why would she be flirting with me if she had a boyfriend?*

Moss walked in the coffee shop, kept his shades on, walked straight up to Derek's table and sat. He grinned, "So, she's meeting you here? This *hot* girl who's into you? Good for you."

Derek shrugged.

"So what's your plan?" Moss asked.

Derek shrugged again. "I don't have one. I don't even know what department she's in."

"You told me she was in Research and Development."

"Yeah. I mean—within that, there's departments," Derek fumbled.

"Calm down. You look good. Relax. Just talk. I'm gonna grab something soy and enjoy the show." Moss knocked on the table, stood and went up to the counter.

Just then, Molly walked in. *Five minutes early.* Derek half-stood and waved. She walked over to the table. They shook hands again and she sat. Derek asked what she wanted and walked up to the counter to order.

He was in line behind Moss, who turned around and nodded at Derek the way a stranger might nod. Then he whispered, barely moving his lips, "Smoking hot!" Derek didn't acknowledge the assessment, waited, ordered drinks, waited some more, watched Moss glance over at Molly on his way to his table, then got their drinks and carried them over to Molly and sat down. She got up to get cream and sugar, then came back to join him.

"Sorry. I should've asked," Derek said.

"Don't worry about it. You must drink yours black. My Daddy drinks black coffee. He told me it puts hair on your chest," she said, stirring her drink. "I've always been a cream and sugar girl."

"Naturally," Derek said and chuckled.

Molly's familiarity didn't seem as flirty in the coffee shop as it had in the office. He felt more comfortable talking to her without people listening and grinning. Moss was there, but he was just staring at the back of her head from across the room—there was no way he could hear what she was saying. Derek felt surprisingly comfortable. "So how long have you worked at Caspian Sea?"

"Eight months? Nine months? Not long."

"And you're in Research and Development?"

"Uh, yeah. That's a little scary," Molly said. "Who told you that?"

"It was a guess," Derek said.

Molly grinned and turned her head slightly.

"Mr. Bensen said it was either that or Marketing."

"How would he know?"

"It's his company," Derek said.

"Yeah, but—" Molly stopped herself and looked around the room over both of her shoulders. She seemed to stop for a second when she saw Moss, who was looking directly at her, though his eyes were hidden behind his shades. She looked back at Derek and leaned in and whispered, "He's a giant mystery."

"The guy with the glasses?" Derek asked.

"Shh!" Molly said and glanced over at Moss who was still look-ing in their direction. She turned back to Derek and, still whispering, asked "That creep? Who's that?"

"I don't know," Derek replied. "Who are you talking about? Who's a mystery?"

"Mr. Bensen."

"What?" Derek asked.

"He doesn't talk to anyone, at least that's what everyone says."

"What do you mean?"

"He's so private. He walks around plenty, but all he does is nod, barely smiles. Some folks think he's mean. I think he might just be really nervous or something. But no one knows anything about him that you can't read in the newspaper.

"He's got a wife. She's pretty. But you never see her, except in photos of them standing together or of her sitting next to him at dinners. At office functions he smiles more, but he doesn't interact with anyone except his wife and the board members. I'm fine with all of that, but I think it's weird that he knows where I work. That's more creepy than his nephew knowing."

"He's not mean and he's not nervous. He's focused, but in a healthy way. What's he supposed to say to people walking around the office? He's working."

"Don't get defensive, I'm just telling you what people think."

"What'd you say about his nephew?" Derek asked.

"I'm just messing with you," Molly said and smiled.

"Huh?"

"Never mind. I was just making a point ... ," she took a sip, then continued, " ... which is—it's surprising that Mr. Bensen would know what department I work in."

"Okay. But you mentioned his nephew. How is he creepy?"

"Geez! Relax. I was kidding. You're sweet. A little intense though."

So many things suddenly made sense to Derek. He sat back in his chair. "Who told you I was Mr. Bensen's nephew?"

"That's just the word," Molly said and tried to explain every-thing. Her explanation was longer than it needed to be with several "she said, I was like, he was like, then I said" twists and turns. Derek grinned from time to time, without laughing or crying. At differ-ent times, he was tempted to do both. Molly explained that people had noticed him coming to the office and meeting with Mr. Bensen regularly. Since it was rare for them to see Mr. Bensen with anyone other than board members and executives, many folks wondered who Derek was. A few people asked Mrs. Howe and she told them he was a college student doing an internship, but no one believed that. They thought it was out of character for any CEO to spend that much time with a random college student. The story developed that Derek was Mr. Bensen's nephew from another part of the country, who'd come to town to study Business at Mr. Bensen's alma mater. He'd shown some kind of promise in business and it was likely that he was being groomed for an executive position and that he'd eventually run the company. It made sense considering the way the employees saw Mr. Bensen as an ultra-private individual, heavily concerned about the future of his business.

As Molly talked, Derek listened and thought. He was able to process why she had been so energetic to offer him a spot on the elevator and why she was so willing to meet him for a cup of coffee. He was somewhat relieved, for Molly's sake, that the grins and head shakes in the office were more likely due to people thinking, *I can't believe the new girl is flirting with Mr. Bensen's nephew* than, *Here goes the cheerleader playing with another boy.* Most importantly, he was able to recover—partially—from the disappointment that Molly would never have looked at him, much less talked to him, if she hadn't thought he was Mr. Bensen's nephew.

The past several weeks had taught him several things about Finance. They'd also taught him a few things about strategy as he tried to sift through the strangeness of the Moss/Stovall/Bensen situ-ation. *If I tell her I'm his nephew, she'd be all embarrassed, possibly angry—she might make a scene—and I'd have no chance of getting any information out of her about the secret ingredients. If I let her keep thinking I'm his nephew, it'd be too weird for me to ask about the recipe, but it gives me leverage. I don't know what to do with that kind of leverage, but I've gotta give myself time to think about it.*

"So, that's how people figured it out," Molly said as she finished her story.

"Makes sense," Derek said. "I think you all might have too much time on your hands. Speaking of—" Derek pulled out his phone and checked the time, "I've gotta be somewhere."

"Really?" Molly asked, and sounded confused. "Okay."

"Yeah, sorry," Derek stood up. "But I'm glad we got to sit and talk. I'm glad I ran into you."

"Me too," Molly said and stood up. "Maybe another cup of coffee soon? The next one's on me?"

"Why not?" Derek said. They shook hands and Derek walked out. He didn't look at Moss.

—

Moss called Derek several times in the hours following the coffee shop meeting with Molly but he didn't answer. He turned his phone off. He gained perspective. After spending time with Molly, he was able to slide in and out of his alter ego as Mr. Bensen's nephew. When he thought as Derek, he was nervous and unsure what to do. When he thought as Mr. Bensen's nephew, things made sense.

I don't owe Moss anything. So what if he arranged to have $10,000 deposited in my account. I'm gonna run this entire company one day. What am I willing to give up today, for what I can have tomorrow, or thirty years from now? Moss says Uncle Eric's into illegal stuff. I can keep my eyes open as he exposes me more to the business. If something stinks, then I'm cautious and when I have *enough information I call the FBI. I'll call the 800 number—stay away from Moss. I can't stand guys who wear sunglasses inside. If Uncle Eric's not illegal I stick with him, keep learning ropes, build my instincts, and I'm running the company one day.*

Derek spent a week processing thoughts as himself and as the nephew. Of course, he knew he had no promise of a future with Caspian Sea, but he felt comfortable with the ethics of the thoughts of his alter ego. After a few days Moss stopped calling. Derek was glad. He hadn't touched the $10,000. He hadn't made any effort to get the secret ingredients from Molly or anyone else. He hadn't done anything wrong. He felt a little guilty about telling Mr. Bensen that he didn't like crowded elevators. *I'll look for a chance to clear that up.*

The following week, Derek felt a comfortable freedom as he rode the elevator up to the 23rd floor. He stepped off, walked in past Mrs. Howe's desk, smiled at a man who walked by and nodded at him like he was the nephew of the CEO, walked into the conference room, put his folder on the table, and sat and stretched and waited for Mr. Bensen, who walked in a minute later.

"How are you, buddy?" Mr. Bensen asked.

"Good," Derek said, "good."

CHAPTER 7

STOCKS:
FEEDING THE CORPORATE MONEY MACHINE II

O k. When Alex and I first formed Caspian Sea Drinks, LLC we needed money," Mr. Bensen said. "We used my credit card and the money we had, but that was not enough. Spencer bought 30% of the company for $40,000. Stovall loaned Caspian Sea $100,000. But remember, Alex and I didn't get that money. Caspian Sea Drinks, LLC got it and used it to buy the equipment and supplies we needed to make enough Caspian Sea to meet the growing demand. That's what small companies do. That's also what big companies like Coke do. In order to raise money to fund growth, a firm will sell equity or debt. Last week we talked about debt. Today we'll talk about equity."

"Okay."

"The payout rule for debt is easy," Mr. Bensen said. "We promised Stovall $108,000, payable in exactly one year. No more, no less—no sooner, no later. The payout rule for stock is not clear. Spencer bought stock in Caspian Sea Drinks, LLC for the same basic reason Stovall bought our "bond." He wanted to make money. Stock is valued by the same rule that values bonds. The value of a share of stock is the present value of its expected future cash flows. The discount rate will be different because the risks are different. The payout rule is different because there is no formal payout rule for stocks."

Mr. Bensen continued, "Spencer became a part owner when he bought stock in Caspian Sea. He was one of us. We had to pay Stovall or he would gain control of the firm."

Derek pictured Stovall as a maniacal Godzilla picking up the building and crashing it into the cityscape. He chuckled.

"What?" Mr. Bensen asked.

"Nothing, just had an image flash in my head. Sorry."

Mr. Bensen sat forward in his chair. "Okay, let's focus. We had to pay Stovall, but we were under no obligation to pay Spencer. He now had a 30% share of the firm. Alex and I had 35% each. Spencer bought in the hope that Alex and I would make wise management decisions that would lead to Caspian Sea becoming a much more valuable company. We did. Spencer is still a shareholder, a very happy shareholder."

"And this Stovall guy. He could have been?" asked Derek.

"What? A happy shareholder? Yeah, I suppose so. But he's not. Why?"

"Nothing," said Derek. "No reason."

"You're all distracted today," Mr. Bensen chuckled. "You need to talk to that girl."

Derek thought it best to say nothing about Molly. "Sorry. So, you said there was no payout rule for Caspian Sea and that Spencer hoped you and Alex would make decisions that would increase Caspian Sea's value. You've drilled it into my head that the value of a financial asset is the present value of the expected future cash flows. If there is no payout rule how can I value the stock? How can I tell if you made decisions that made it increase in value?"

"Good question. You're with me," Mr. Bensen said. "That's good. We'll start with stocks that have payout rules. Cash payments from stocks are called dividends. Unlike the coupon payments of bonds, management of a company can change the dividend at any time. Companies don't like to lower the dividend. Normally, they raise it only if they know they will have enough earnings in the future to pay the higher dividend. Make sense?"

"Yeah, I think," Derek said.

"Assume Caspian Sea Drinks is still a publicly traded corporation, like Coke. Caspian Sea pays dividends once per year and just paid a $2.00 dividend earlier today. As CEO, I've announced that we intend to continue paying dividends once per year. An analyst can make some simple assumptions and come up with the precise value of Caspian Sea Drinks. It's just the present value of the future expected cash flows." Mr. Bensen stood and wrote on the board.

$$P_0 = \frac{D_1}{(1 + k)^1} + \frac{D_2}{(1 + k)^2} + \frac{D_3}{(1 + k)^3} + \frac{D_4}{(1 + k)^4} + \frac{D_5}{(1 + k)^5} + \cdots$$

"Stop," Derek said. "If Caspian Sea stays in business forever, then they'll pay a dividend every year forever. I can't find the present value of an infinite series of cash flows. There has to be a shortcut."

"Relax. There is. All we have to do is make one simplifying assumption and use one cool algebra trick. Rather than trying to *guesstimate* an exact value for each dividend for the next thousand years and beyond, assume the dividend will grow at a constant rate. Then ... " He wrote on the board again.

$$P_0 = \frac{D_1}{k - g}$$

"assume an analyst, call him Joseph, believes the dividend will grow at 5% and the cost of equity is 12%. We'll talk about why he believes that later. For now just get up and do the math."

Derek stood and wrote on the board.

$$D_1 = D_0(1 + g) = 2.00*1.05 = 2.10$$

$$P_0 = \frac{2.10}{0.12 - 0.05} = 30.00$$

"The math is easy," Derek said. "Now that I know how to value them, can I make a bunch of money trading stocks?"

"No. You only know one theoretical construct. You've assumed dividends will grow at a constant rate of 5% forever. You've assumed the appropriate discount rate is 12%. You might be wrong. What if everybody else thinks the growth rate was 4%?

"Then the value would be ... " Derek wrote on the board.

$$D_1 = D_0(1 + g) = 2.00*1.04 = 2.08$$

$$P_0 = \frac{2.08}{0.12 - 0.04} = 26.00$$

Mr. Bensen looked at the board and said, "So you would have paid $30.00 for a stock everybody else thinks is only worth $26.00. If you're right, you just got a great deal. If you're wrong, you just got ripped off. Only time will tell. Investors are constantly changing their estimates for k and g based on new information, which means the price is constantly changing. They may even be rethinking the idea that the dividend will grow at a constant rate. In that case they may switch to another model—one where the dividend does not grow at a constant rate.

"Maybe an analyst will look at a company and think that dividends will grow at a faster-than-normal rate for the next three years and slow down to a normal growth rate after that," Mr. Bensen said. "If that's the case, then finding the value of the firm is a little more involved. It's the same principle—the value of the firm is the present value of the expected future cash flows—it's just that the cash flows (the dividends) don't grow at a nice constant rate forever.

"Here's an example," he continued. "Assume another analyst, Abby, looks at Caspian Sea. Like the first analyst, she can see the company just paid a dividend of $2.00. She thinks that the dividend will grow at 20% for the next three years and then settle down to grow at 5% forever. The appropriate discount rate is still assumed to be 12%. Who do you think will pay more for the stock? Why? Exactly how much will Abby pay?

"I'd say Abby will pay more because she thinks the dividends will be higher than Joseph does. Let me take a shot at the math." Derek wrote on the board.

$$P_0 = \frac{D_1}{(1+k)^1} + \frac{D_2}{(1+k)^2} + \frac{D_3}{(1+k)^3} + \frac{P_3}{(1+k)^3}$$
$$and \ P_3 = \frac{D_4}{k-g}$$

"The rule is: the price of the stock is equal to the present value of the expected future cash flows," Derek continued. "This means I have to discount an infinite number of dividends. But if the dividends grow at a constant rate, there's a math trick that makes the calculation easy. So, I have to discount the dividends in the high growth period individually. Then I can use the constant growth formula in year three."

$$D_1 = 2.00*1.20 = 2.4000$$

$$D_2 = 2.44*1.20 = 2.8800$$

$$D_3 = 2.88*1.20 = 3.4560$$

"Now I need D_4 so I can find P_3."

$$D_4 = 3.4560*1.05 = 3.6288$$
$$P_3 = \frac{3.6288}{0.12 - 0.05} = 51.84$$
$$P_0 = \frac{2.40}{(1.12)^1} + \frac{2.88_2}{(1.12)^2} + \frac{3.456}{(1.12)^3} + \frac{51.84}{(1.12)^3} = 43.80$$

"I look at it this way: I can hold the stock for three years and get the dividends. After three years I can sell it. Whoever I sell it to cares only about the future dividends. To this new buyer, Caspian Sea is a constant growth stock, so he or she will value it using the constant growth model. My four cash flows are the three dividends plus the money I get from selling the stock. I have to be careful when I do the math because I get the last dividend and sell the stock on the same day. So I discount both back three years. *And*, $43.80 is a lot more than $30.00."

"You got it," Mr. Bensen said. An old, wise analyst once told me that you can never win on *the Finance*. You can only lose. You win on your assumptions and being able to defend them. You're learning *the Finance*. You're learning the math behind these models and what the models mean. Anybody can plug numbers into a calculator and solve the equations. The hard part is knowing what numbers to put into the formula."

"Abby will advise her clients to buy Caspian Sea if the price is below $43.80. Joseph will advise his clients to sell if the price is above $30.00. Their advice is based in part on what they believe the future dividends will be. Next year they'll find out who was closest to D_1."

"Closest?" Derek asked.

"Yeah. Chances are they're both wrong, but they'll find out who was closest to the truth. One set of clients will win, the other set will lose. The winner smiles big and the loser gulps and tries to explain why the assumptions were made.

"The question is: *How did Abby and Joseph estimate* k *and* g? Let's start with k. k is the *Cost of Equity* or the *Discount Rate* or the *Required Rate of Return*. Think about the names. If Caspian Sea or any other company wants to raise money, they can't get people to donate like it's a charity. They have to give the new investors a piece of the pie. In this case, that's a claim on the future dividends of the firm. That cost is represented in percentage terms. The potential

CHAPTER 7

investors will discount the future dividends like you just did. In order to invest in a particular company, you require a certain return. Here's how you decide exactly what that required return will be.

"You said you'd pay more for a money machine that pays out a certain amount—*guaranteed*—than you would for one with a risky payout. Treasury securities are guaranteed money machines. Stocks are risky ones. Call the return on a Treasury the *Risk-free Rate*. To induce you to buy a stock, you must get the *Risk-free Rate* plus a *Risk Premium*. Estimating the *Risk Premium* is probably the hardest part of finding k in real life. There are different ways to do it. We'll use something called the *Capital Asset Pricing Model*—lots of folks call it the *cap-m*." Mr. Bensen wrote on the board. This time he referred regularly to a sheet he'd left sitting on the table.

The CAPM

$$k_{CSD} = r_f + \beta_{CSD}\left[E(r_m) - r_f\right]$$

"Can't get in a hurry writing that stuff. You recognize any of those symbols?"

"Should I?" asked Derek.

Mr. Bensen didn't answer. "The required return for Caspian Sea, k_{CSD}, equals the *Risk-free Rate*, r_f, plus a *Risk Premium*. The *Risk Premium* has two components, β_{CSD}, and the *Market Risk Premium*. β_{CSD} is the relationship of Caspian Sea and the market. The *Market Risk Premium* is the expected return on the market minus the *Risk-free Rate*.

"Okay," said Derek, as if it was a question.

"Think of it this way," Mr. Bensen said. "How much extra return do you need to get to buy a stock with average risk instead of a risk-less security? That's the *Market Risk Premium*. Next, is Caspian Sea a relatively risky stock or a relatively safe stock? That's what β_{CSD} tells you." He watched Derek's face for a few seconds. "You're either confused or you're still thinking about the girl. Take this stuff home and work on it. It'll make sense. If not, ask me more next week."

Derek took a deep breath while shaking his head, and exhaled. Mr. Bensen patted him on the back and headed out of the room.

Study Packet: Stocks

Definitions

Preferred Stock is a hybrid security. It has some characteristics of debt and some of common stock. It pays a dividend like common stock. Unlike common stock the dividend is fixed and will never increase. Bondholders and preferred stockholders are both promised a series of future cash flows. The cash flows for preferred stock will continue forever while bond payments have a maturity date. (Perpetual pay bonds have been issued in the past but are extremely rare.) Therefore, both bondholders and preferred stockholders are only interested in the company performing well enough to generate the promised cash flows. If a promised dividend payment is missed, the firm does not enter bankruptcy but it cannot pay a dividend to common stockholders until the preferred stockholders are made whole. Preferred shareholders do not have voting rights.

Common Stock is sometimes called equity. Common stockholders are the owners of the firm. They are called the residual claimants since they are entitled to all the cash flows of the firm after all other stakeholders are paid. Management must decide when the dividend will be paid and how much it will be. Common shareholders elect a board of directors. The board hires and possibly fires management. In some cases firms issue a class of common stock that has voting rights and a class that does not.

Unless otherwise noted, all dividends are assumed to be paid annually with the next dividend to be paid in exactly one year. This assumption makes learning stock valuation easier. In practice, firms may pay according to any schedule they wish and the math needed to value a firm is not significantly different.

Equations

$$(3.2) \qquad PVA_n = pmt * \left[\frac{1 - \frac{1}{(1+i)^n}}{i} \right]$$

Recall equation 3.2. Remember that the price of any financial asset is the present value of the expected future cash flows. The cash flows for preferred stock are expected to continue forever. That means n equals infinity. Letting n go to infinity gives the following equation:

$$(7.1) \qquad P_{PS} = \frac{D}{k}$$

where P_{PS} is the price of preferred stock, D is the promised dividend and k is the required rate of return on preferred stock.

Since common stock pays a dividend forever its price is given by:

$$(7.2) \qquad P_0 = \frac{D_1}{(1+k)^1} + \frac{D_2}{(1+k)^2} + \frac{D_3}{(1+k)^3} + \frac{D_4}{(1+k)^4} + \frac{D_5}{(1+k)^5} + \cdots$$

If we assume that dividends grow at a constant rate, g, forever then we know:

$$D_1 = D_0(1 + g)^1$$

In general:

(7.3) $$D_{n+t} = D_n(1 + g)^t$$

Equation 7.3 follows from equation 2.1. We can now say:

$$P_0 = \frac{D_1}{(1 + k)^1} + \frac{D_1(1 + g)}{(1 + k)^2} + \frac{D_1(1 + g)^2}{(1 + k)^3} + \cdots$$

$$\frac{1 + k}{1 + g}P_0 = \frac{D_1}{(1 + k)^1} + \frac{D_1(1 + g)}{(1 + k)^2} + \frac{D_1(1 + g)^2}{(1 + k)^3} + \cdots$$

$$\frac{1 + k}{1 + g}P_0 - P_0 = \frac{D_1}{(1 + g)^1}$$

(7.4) $$P_0 = \frac{D_1}{k - g}$$

It is extremely important to recognize the assumptions made in deriving equation 7.4. The next dividend will be paid in exactly one year. Equation 7.4 is the same as equation 7.2 if the dividends grow at a constant rate. It gives the present value of the future cash flows.

PROBLEM SET

1. A firm issues preferred stock with a dividend of $2.00. If the appropriate discount rate is 10%, what is the value of the preferred stock?

2. The market price of a share of preferred stock is $19.20 and the dividend is $2.40. What discount rate did the market use to value the stock?

3. The market price of a share of preferred stock is $18.75. The market uses a discount rate of 8.00%. What is the dividend?

4. Caspian Sea is considering raising $25 million by issuing preferred stock. They believe the market will use a discount rate of 13.00% to value the preferred stock that will pay a dividend of $2.60. How many shares will they need to issue?

5. Repeat question 4 assuming a dividend of $3.90. Does it matter to Caspian Sea what the dividend is or how many shares they sell?

6. A firm will pay a dividend of $1.26 next year. The dividend is expected to grow at a constant rate of 5.00% forever and the required rate of return is 15.00%. What is the value of the stock?

7. A firm just paid a dividend of $1.26. The dividend is expected to grow at a constant rate of 5.00% forever and the required rate of return is 15.00%. What is the value of the stock? Notice the difference in the wording of this question and that of question 6. Which stock is worth more? Why?

8. A firm will pay a dividend of $1.50 next year. The dividend is expected to grow at a constant rate of 4.50% forever and the required rate of return is 14.00%. What is the value of the stock?

9. A firm just paid a dividend of $1.20. The dividend is expected to grow at a constant rate of 3.00% forever and the required rate of return is 12.00%. What is the value of the stock?

10. The market price of a stock is $20.00 and it is expected to pay a $2.00 dividend next year. The dividend is expected to grow at 5% forever. What is the required rate of return for the stock?

11. The market price of a stock is $50.00 and it just paid $5.25 dividend. The dividend is expected to grow at 4% forever. What is the required rate of return for the stock?

12. The market price of a stock is $30.00 and it is expected to pay a dividend of $2.50 next year. The required rate of return is 12%. What is the expected growth rate of the dividend?

13. The market price of a stock is $62.40 and it just paid a dividend of $6.00. The required rate of return is 14%. What is the expected growth rate of the dividend?

14. Can the growth rate of the dividend ever be higher than the discount rate?

15. Can the growth rate of the dividend remain above the growth rate of the economy forever?

16. A stock just paid a dividend of $2.50. The dividend is expected to grow at 20% for three years and then grow at 5% thereafter. The required return on the stock is 12%. What is the value of the stock?

17. A stock just paid a dividend of $1.20. The dividend is expected to grow at 25% for five years and then grow at 3% thereafter. The required return on the stock is 15%. What is the value of the stock?

18. A stock just paid a dividend of $4.00. The dividend is expected to grow at 30% for two years and then grow at 4.5% thereafter. The required return on the stock is 13.6%. What is the value of the stock?

19. The risk-free rate is 2.00% and the market risk premium is 5.50%. A stock with a β of 1.10 will have an expected return of ____%.

20. The risk-free rate is 3.00% and the expected return on the market 9.75%. A stock with a β of 0.80 will have an expected return of ____%.
21. A stock has an expected return of 17%. The risk-free rate is 3% and the market risk premium is 10%. What is the β of the stock?
22. The risk-free rate is 2.50% and the market risk premium is 6.00%. A stock with a β of 1.20 just paid a dividend of $3.00. The dividend is expected to grow at 20% for three years and then grow at 4.00% forever. What is the value of the stock?
23. The risk-free rate is 3.50% and the market risk premium is 7.00%. A stock with a β of 1.50 just paid a dividend of $5.00. The dividend is expected to grow at 15% for five years and then grow at 5.00% forever. What is the value of the stock?
24. Caspian Sea Drinks needs to raise $50 million by issuing additional shares of stock. If the market estimates CSD will pay a dividend of $1.00 which will grow at 4.00% forever and the cost of equity to be 12.0%, then how many shares of stock must CSD sell? What are the advantages and disadvantages of issuing stock rather than bonds to raise the needed capital?
25. Suppose the risk-free rate is 2.00% and an analyst assumes the market risk premium is 4.50%. Firm A just paid a dividend of $1.25 per share. The analyst estimates the β of Firm A to be 1.30 and estimates dividend growth of 5.0% forever. Firm A has 200 million shares outstanding. Firm B just paid a dividend of $1.50 per share. The analyst estimates the β of Firm B is 0.90 and estimates dividend growth of 3.0% forever. Firm B has 120 million shares. Which firm is more valuable?

7.1

Derek was happy to feel overwhelmed by something other than thoughts of Moss or Molly or Stovall or secret ingredients. He poked his head out of the conference room door and looked left down the hall to make sure Molly wasn't looking or heading his way. She wasn't. He walked out, quickly, past Mrs. Howe and out to the elevators.

He hadn't talked to Moss since their conversation in the coffee shop the week before. He'd be happy to never see or hear from Moss again, but he didn't figure that was possible. Thinking he'd probably have to have at least one more confrontation with Moss, Derek wanted to get it over with. He was prepared. If Moss wasn't outside the building, he'd go to the park. If he wasn't in the park, Derek would call him and arrange a meeting. If he didn't want to meet, Derek would tell him over the phone. He had it all planned out.

I'm out. I'm done. I'm sorry. I'm not any good at this stuff and I'm not going to keep trying. I'm an intern, getting a valuable education. I'll give Stovall back his money. I haven't touched it. Again, I'm sorry.

No Moss outside the building. No Moss in the park. Moss didn't answer his phone. Derek sat on the bench, still confident. He called four times in thirty minutes before he finally decided to leave a voice mail. He said what he had to say, hung up, turned his phone off, stood up and walked out of the park, smiling.

—

Derek spent a few hours working through the Study Packet and getting his head around the nuanced ways stocks fit into the money machine. He was pleased to see how focused he could be when he wasn't thinking about espionage. Other than the sinister smile he'd seen reflected in the window, which could have been so many things, he had no reason to think Mr. Bensen was anything but a really good guy. The less he thought about Moss and Stovall and their accusations, the more comfortable he felt about Mr. Bensen.

When he walked by Mrs. Howe's desk the next Wednesday, she said, "Derek. Hello. I have a note here. Molly left it for you. Do you two know each other?"

"Molly," Derek said. "Yeah, I mean a little."

"Nice girl," Mrs. Howe said and handed him an envelope. "Pretty girl."

Derek took the envelope and said, "Thanks. Down the hall?"

"Yup, he just went that way," Mrs. Howe said.

Derek wanted to open the envelope. He thought about ducking into the bathroom quickly, but he didn't want to appear to be late. He put the envelope into his folder. *Forget about it. Literally, forget about it. You'll remember it when you get home to do the homework.* He walked into the conference room where Mr. Bensen was seated.

"Hey, have a seat. I've got a good story for you," Mr. Bensen said.

Derek gulped.

CHAPTER 8

CAPITAL BUDGETING 1:
GROWING THE CORPORATE MONEY MACHINE

I n the early days of Caspian Sea, Alex and I used to make the stuff in my kitchen by hand. It took us all day and we were never able to make as much as we wanted. And it wrecked my kitchen. Half of the work was cleaning up. But we didn't have another option so we just did it. Then Alex came back from a weekend at a family reunion. He didn't have a car so he'd gotten a ride home with his uncle. I'm sitting on the couch and hear this banging on the door. I get up and open it and his uncle's back fills the doorway. He just about ran over me. He and Alex were carrying this huge copper drum kind of thing—somehow got lucky with the angle and got it through the door—and Alex was on the other end of it shouting, 'Back, back, straight back! Keep going!' When they got to the kitchen they dropped it in the middle of the floor. They stood up and Alex tells me, 'Here we go! This is our Caspian machine—it's a mixer. No more sinks and buckets.' Then he tells me we owe his uncle $1,000 for it. His uncle didn't say a word the whole visit. I looked at him and grinned and he just stared at me. I found out later his uncle needed a lawyer—he'd been making something he shouldn't make out of the thing that was now taking up my kitchen. Who knows how much he paid for the thing, if he ever paid for it? He needed $1,000 for the lawyer, so that's what he was charging us for the machine. So, how should we decide whether or not to buy it?"

"It's a money machine," Derek answered. "It's also a still," he said out of the side of his mouth."

"It's a mixer. Let's call it a mixer," Mr. Bensen said, without grinning.

"Okay. What are the size, timing, and risks of the cash flows? The mixer costs $1,000. If the present value of the future expected cash flows are greater than $1,000 then you should buy it. But what are the cash flows it generates?"

"Good question. I'll give you a more detailed answer later," Mr. Bensen said. "You'll even have to calculate the cash flows on your own. For now, just think about the big picture. The mixer will make more Caspian Sea faster so we can sell more product. We assumed that after costs we'd make $500 a year more than if we didn't have it. We also assumed the mixer would last only three years. After considering the risk, we decided the appropriate discount rate was 12%. Take a shot and work through it on the board."

Derek stood and wrote:

$$\frac{500}{1.12^1} + \frac{500}{1.12^2} + \frac{500}{1.12^3} = 1,200.92$$

"So, the present value of the cash flows is greater than the cost. Buy it," Derek said.

"You're right, but let me put that in more formal Finance language. We're looking for the *Net Present Value* of the project. Most folks call it the *NPV* of the project." Mr. Bensen wrote on the board.

$$NPV = -1,000 + \frac{500}{1.12^1} + \frac{500}{1.12^2} + \frac{500}{1.12^3} = 200.92$$

"Okay. A few things to recognize here. First, common sense tells you to do something if the pros outweigh the cons, right? That's not Finance—that's life. For us, the cons are spending $1,000 to buy the mixer and the pros are the future cash flows. Second, the formal decision rule is this: accept the project if the NPV is greater than zero;

reject the project if the NPV is less than zero. Third, the benefits were $200.92 higher than the costs. That means we increased the value of Caspian Sea by $200.92 by buying the mixer. Fourth, we didn't know any of this junk. We bought the mixer because it seemed like a good idea—I was sick of spending every weekend wrecking and cleaning up my kitchen; also, I didn't like the idea of trying to tell Alex's sweating, scowling uncle *no*.

"Now, when you did that calculation, you assumed the $500 cash flows started in exactly one year. I never told you that." Mr. Bensen paused and looked at Derek. Derek didn't say anything. "I told you that we'd make $500 more per year. We sold Caspian Sea every day. Why did you assume the timing that you did?"

"I don't know," Derek said. "Habit? I didn't even think about it."

"To keep this as simple as possible let's assume that the cash flows occur in one big payment at the end of each year. Just remember that's not reality. Reality is messy. You've gotta learn a simpler version of it first. Make sure you understand what we're doing here. Caspian Sea is trying to decide if they should accept a project. By *project* I mean buy a mixer, hire some people, build a plant, or whatever. They have to estimate the size, timing, and risk of the cash flows. For now, I'll tell you what the cash flows are and when they occur. I'll also tell you the discount rate. The discount rate accounts for the risk of the cash flows. The greater the risk, the higher the discount rate; the higher the discount rate, the lower the NPV.

"Here's rule number 1," Mr. Bensen said and wrote on the board.

$$NPV = -CF_0 + \frac{CF_1}{(1+k)^1} + \frac{CF_2}{(1+k)^2} + \frac{CF_3}{(1+k)^3} + \cdots + \frac{CF_n}{(1+k)^n}$$

If NPV > 0 accept

NPV < 0 reject

NPV = 0 indifferent

"Okay? It doesn't matter if it's two guys thinking about buying a mixer or a multi-billion dollar corporation considering the construction of a new plant—the principle is the same."

"Got it," Derek said.

"There are, of course, more rules," Mr. Bensen said. "We'll look at one more. It's called IRR, or *Internal Rate of Return*. What if k was 25% for the project we just did?"

Derek wrote on the board.

$$NPV = -1,000 + \frac{500}{1.25^1} + \frac{500}{1.25^2} + \frac{500}{1.25^3} = -24.00$$

"Okay. So here, we shouldn't accept the project."

"Correct. Notice that a higher k made the NPV lower. In reality, k is difficult to estimate. I'm not sure if it should be 12.00% or 12.12%. So I do the following. Try to find the value for k that makes NPV = 0. We started with 12% and NPV was greater than zero. So we raised k to 25%. Why 25%? I just picked a number higher than 12%. If k = 25% then NPV is less than zero. That means we should lower k. Finally after hours of guessing, or seconds of pushing the right buttons on a calculator, we find that k = 23.375%, making NPV = 0.

"That number, 23.375%, is the IRR. It means that if k is less than 23.375% then NPV will be greater than zero and we should accept the project. So the IRR rule is," Mr. Bensen wrote on the board.

IRR > k accept

IRR < k reject

"Folks sometimes call k the hurdle rate. It is the cost of capital. If the IRR is greater than my cost of capital then I should do the project. Note the terminology. If the return is greater than the cost then you do it. IRR has to get over the hurdle."

"You mentioned the calculator," Derek said. "What buttons do I push to get IRR?"

"The study packet will explain all that," Mr. Bensen said. "Do you see the big picture? That's the main thing. What we did today is called *Capital Budgeting* in Finance-speak. Caspian Sea or any company has to know if doing one of these projects is worth it. They either create or destroy firm value. My job is to ... " Mr. Bensen paused for Derek to finish his sentence.

"Make money," Derek said quickly. "Maximize shareholder wealth."

"Yes. So, I need to find positive NPV projects—projects that create wealth. If potential investors like the projects I'm undertaking, then they will want to buy the stock. The more people who want to buy the stock, the higher the stock price goes, and the happier my current shareholders are. If potential investors don't like the projects ... " Mr. Bensen paused. "Well ... obviously ...

"Okay. Work through these problems. Get the math down cold. There's a twist or two in this week's problem set. I want to see if you can handle them. There are some important concept questions, too. This stuff's not easy. Good luck. See you next week."

STUDY PACKET: PROJECTS

Comments

In addition to NPV and IRR, managers sometimes use *payback period*, *discounted payback period*, or *profitability index*. The following example illustrates the different approaches to evaluating a project. Assume the cash flows given below and a cost of capital of 10%.

For simplicity purposes the cash flows of every project will be assumed to occur in annual increments. In reality, construction costs for a plant will be spread over time. Revenues and costs will perhaps occur on a daily basis. It is important to learn the fundamentals before considering more complicated yet realistic cash flows.

NPV and IRR give the same accept/reject decision with one important exception. The typical project will have an initial cost, which means CF0 is negative. All the following cash flows will be positive. However, this may not always be the case. If one or more future cash flows is negative, then there may be more than one IRR that make NPV equal to zero. In these cases, use NPV to evaluate the project and ignore IRR.

Year	CF
0	-10,000
1	3,000
2	3,000
3	2,000
4	2,500
5	5,000

The financial calculator will make calculating NPV and IRR quick and easy if you carefully follow these instructions.

Entering cash flows

1. Press 'CF', then 2nd, then CLRWRK. Do this before beginning each problem to clear information from previous work.
2. Key in the value -10,000, then press ENTER. This is CF0.
3. Press '↓' then 3,000, then ENTER.
4. Press '↓' and 2 for F01, then ENTER. This tells the calculator that the $3,000 cash flow occurs twice.
5. Press '↓' then 2,000, then ENTER.
6. Press '↓' and 1 for F02, then ENTER. This tells the calculator that the $2,000 cash flow occurs one time.
7. Press '↓' then 2,500, then ENTER.
8. Press '↓' and 1 for F03, then ENTER.
9. Press '↓' then 5,000, then ENTER.
10. Press '↓' and 1 for F04, then ENTER. Now the calculator knows the cash flow you want to evaluate.

IRR—Press 'IRR' then 'CPT'. The IRR equals 15.4262%.

NPV—press 'NPV' and enter 10 for the discount rate. Press 'ENTER' then '↓' then 'CPT'. The NPV should be $1,521.38

Payback period—the number of years needed to recover the initial investment. In this example, you will recover $8,000 after three years. In year four you receive $2,500 but only need $2,000 to recover the full $10,000. Therefore, the payback period is 3 + 2,000/2,500 or 3.8 years.

The payback period approach has three weaknesses. First, it does not have a formal accept/reject rule. Is 3.8 years too long to wait? How about 3.5 years? Second, it does not take into account the time value of money. Third, it does not consider the cash flows after the payback period is over. Imagine a project identical to the one above except the cash flow in year 5 is $100,000. Clearly you prefer the latter project but the payback period approach makes no distinction between the projects. The approach is only useful for quick "back of the envelope" calculations.

Discounted payback period—identical to the payback period except you use the present value of the future cash flows to calculate the payback period.

Year	CF	PV(CF)	Sum of PV(CF)
0	-10,000	-10,000.00	
1	3,000	2,727.27	2,727.27
2	3,000	2,479.34	5,206.61
3	2,000	1,502.63	6,709.24
4	2,500	1,707.53	8,416.77
5	5,000	3,104.61	11,521.38

The discounted payback period is 4 + 1,583.23/3,104.61 = 4.51 years.

Profitability index—gives the value of the benefits of the project relative to the costs.

$$PI = \frac{PV(benefits)}{PV(\cos ts)} = \frac{NPV + initialCF}{initialCF}$$

If the PI is greater than one, then the NPV was positive.

PROBLEM SET

1. Caspian Sea Drinks is considering buying the J-Mix 2000. It will allow them to make and sell more product. The machine cost $1 million and will increase cash flows by $320,000 each year for the next five years. The cost of capital is 9.34%. Find the NPV, IRR, PI, payback period and discounted payback period of buying the machine. What does this mean for the value of Caspian Sea Drinks?

2. Repeat #1 using 25% for cost of capital. What happened to the NPV? PI? Payback period? Discount payback period?

3. Find the NPV, IRR, and PI for each of the following projects. Assume a cost of capital of 10%, Repeat using a cost of capital of 15%, then 20%. What will happen to the NPV, IRR, and PI of the projects as the cost of capital increases? Does it appear that an accurate estimate of the cost of capital is important?

Year	Project A	Project B	Project C	Project D	Project E
0	-100,000	-73,000	-90,000	-100,000	-170,000
1	18,000	19,500	20,000	20,000	52,500
2	18,000	19,500	25,000	-25,000	52,500
3	18,000	19,500	40,000	100,000	52,500
4	18,000	19,500	50,000	-25,000	52,500
5	18,000	37,000		100,000	52,500
6	18,000				52,500
7	18,000				73,000
8	18,000				
9	18,000				
10	18,000				

8.1

Derek looked down the hall to his left again when leaving the conference room. This time, part of him was hoping he would see Molly. She obviously wanted to speak to him about something. But the other part of him knew there was a good chance she wanted to talk to him because of who she thought he was—and he didn't want to have another enigmatic conversation where he lets her think what she wants. He looked, no Molly.

He was going to open the envelope on the elevator, but there were a few people—Caspian Sea people—riding down with him. He didn't want them reading over his shoulder—he felt odd enough knowing they were probably thinking he was Mr. Bensen's nephew. He was glad no one talked to him. As soon as he stepped off the elevator, he saw Molly. She ran up to him, looking both desperate and sheepish. "Okay. I know I'm an idiot. I can't imagine what you think about me," she said.

"What? First of all, let's walk—people are moving here."

"Okay," she began walking beside him, but kept looking at his face. "But please hear me out. I'm gonna quit, if I don't get fired. But I need to talk to you first. I don't know where to start. Did you read my note? Did you get it? I gave it to Mrs. Howe."

They walked out of the building and onto the sidewalk. Derek pointed across the street at the coffee shop. "You got time? Let's sit and talk."

Molly nodded. They crossed, then Derek held the door open. A few heads turned as he'd visualized a few weeks earlier. It didn't have the effect he imagined it would. Derek was happy to see that none of the faces, turning or otherwise, was Moss's.

Molly walked over to the same table they'd sat at before. Derek ordered drinks. *Last time she said drinks would be on her. I won't remind her of that.* He brought the drinks to the table, this time with cream and sugar. Molly thanked him, but not in a way that made him think she was aware that he had remembered the cream and sugar. Molly poured and stirred. Like before, Derek sat so he could see the rest of the room behind her head.

"I haven't read the note," Derek said. "I got it, but haven't had a chance to read it."

"It doesn't matter," Molly said and dropped the stirring stick and covered her face with her hands. Derek was afraid she was crying. She wasn't. She took her hands down and took a sip. "Okay. First of all, I'm sorry. I know you know it already, but I only talked to you because I thought you were Mr. Bensen's nephew. I mean, I only talked to you the way I did because of that. I don't flirt with every guy I talk to, I promise. But it's sort of a default when I feel threatened. I grew up in pageants." Molly stopped talking and looked out the window. "There are some really mean people working up there. They told me the whole thing about you being Mr. Bensen's nephew, and they were all in on it. The whole thing is they wanted to see what I'd do—they placed bets—they wouldn't tell me how much the winner won. It's awful." Molly's bottom lip trembled as she spoke and tears suddenly filled her eyes. She paused for a second and dabbed at her eyes with a napkin. "Sorry. I was a cheerleader. I liked football. I liked my friends. But there are some mean people up there—*bullies*. They had me all set up to be the office skank just because I used to be a cheerleader. I thought this kind of thing just happened to a few unlucky kids in middle school." Molly was sobbing. She blew her nose.

If you blew your nose like that in middle school you could've been one of those unlucky kids, Derek thought. He felt bad for her. "I should've told you," he said.

"Well, maybe," Molly said, sniffling. "But I know you had to be pretty angry too. I don't blame you."

"It wasn't that, really," Derek said. "So when did they tell you?"

"They *didn't*. Listen. You remember that creepy guy with the shades?"

Derek felt his skin get hot and he swallowed hard, "Yeah. The guy who was in here when we had coffee?"

"Yeah. So you left—and I can understand why you left now—I still had coffee to drink. That guy came over and he was all, 'what's a sweetheart like you doin' in a dump like this?' and all. Gross. But I was nice to him. Again, when I get nervous I flirt. It's awful. I hate it. I told him I was meeting you, mentioned that you were Mr. Bensen's nephew. He said he didn't know who Mr. Bensen was. I explained everything about Caspian Sea and all. He asked what kind of work I did and we talked a bit. He wasn't horrible or anything, just creepy. But, after a while, it's like a switch went off. He asked me why I thought you were Mr. Bensen's nephew. I told him. He told me you were working for him—that he was a federal agent investigating Caspian Sea—and you were doing inside work for him. He told me you were dangerous and lazy and asked if I wanted to earn some extra money doing what you weren't able to do—maybe do some traveling. He asked me if I'd ever been to the Caspian Sea. I told him I was fine with my job. He told me the government was willing to pay a ton of money for some documentation about the drink's ingredients and asked how hard it would be for me to access it. I told him I wasn't comfortable talking about that stuff with him. He got impatient, gave me his card, and told me to call him when I thought about the money and the Caspian Sea."

"Wow. Sorry," Derek said.

Molly dabbed her eyes and blew her nose again. She looked at Derek.

"Okay. So you wanted to tell me that?" he asked.

"Well, yeah. I didn't know what to do for a few days. I felt horrible. I hoped like crazy I wouldn't see you at work and that no one would see me talking to you and no one would ask me if we had coffee. You know they were all watching when we met that day in the office."

Derek nodded.

"The next day a girl asked me if we'd gone out. I explained to her we'd just had a quick cup of coffee. I thought about telling her that someone else told me you weren't Mr. Bensen's nephew, but I didn't want to get in trouble for speaking to this agent guy—something about talking to him made me feel guilty. So I didn't say anything else. No one said anything for a few days. Then, a guy who'd been on vacation—a real tool—came back to work and asked me all kinds of questions about my night with Bensen's nephew. I don't know why but I said I didn't think you were Bensen's nephew. He stood up at his desk and looked around at everyone with his arms out and announced, 'Molly figured it out! I promise I didn't tell her.' That's when they explained the whole thing to me. I took two days off. Today was my first day back. It was humiliating. People are still snickering and shaking their heads at me. The only thing I knew I had to do was try to talk to you today."

Derek felt genuine sympathy for Molly, but he was unsure of what he could or should do next. "I'm glad you talked to me. You're right, those folks sound pretty bad. I don't know what else to say."

"Talk to me," Molly said, bothered. "Give me some kind of explanation. Who are you really? Do you know that guy? Don't tell me you're Mr. Bensen's nephew or I'll scream."

Derek wasn't sure what to share and what not to. He'd been watching the door and the windows but there was no sign of Moss. He decided to try the whole truth. *Sounds like that's what she's doing.* He leaned and talked quietly, though not whispering. "Okay. I'm a college kid doing an internship kind of thing with Mr. Bensen. We meet once a week and he's teaching me some Finance stuff. He's a nice guy—I met him at a benefit thing. Your boy with the shades is Moss. He says he's a government agent. He's been on me for a couple of months trying to get me to get the ingredients for Caspian Sea. I guess—I'm realizing this as I'm telling you—*I'm* the one who owes *you* an apology. *I* was looking for *you* that day, but partly—mostly— because I wanted to talk to you to get Moss off my back. I told him I knew a girl who worked in Research and Development. I figured I'd talk to you and see what happened. That's it."

"Huh," Molly said and looked out the window. "You were playing me. That makes me feel better." She took a drink. "So what do we do now?"

"I'm not sure we have to do anything," Derek said. "After hearing all this, I trust Moss less than ever. I don't know who he is, but he's not an agent. Not if he's talking to you about me offering you money."

"You think he's into some illegal stuff?"

"If he's not an agent and he's saying he is—that's illegal. Who knows what else he might be into?"

"You know, when I started, part of the orientation for Research and Development staff is telling us how to handle people who are asking about our products. They tell us what to say and they tell us to report the person if we think it's someone who's really trying to steal ideas. You think I should report him?"

"If that's what they tell you to do, yeah. Absolutely. But here's the thing. First of all, don't quit. You said something about quitting earlier. Don't. Who's your ultimate supervisor?" Derek asked.

"Dr. Bloom. He's a research scientist guy. Seems okay," Molly said.

"Was he in on the whole nephew thing?"

"No—as far as I know."

"Okay. Go to him and tell him about Moss. Tell him the whole thing start to finish—try to do it without crying. He'll listen to the whole thing and, if he's any good, he'll know the best way to handle the whole bullying situation. Don't quit because of a bunch of morons. Also, he'll be impressed that you were conscientious enough to do your job and report that someone was asking about ingredients, and he'll know what to do, if anything, about Moss."

"Derek. Thank you," Molly said. Her eyes teared up again. "Really. Thank you."

"You're welcome. I'm sorry I didn't help you out more when I could have."

"No, you're helping now. You're a good person. I'm really sorry for the flirting and all of that. Really. I am."

"Don't worry about it," Derek said. "Seriously. Talk to this Bloom guy, tomorrow. Let me know how it works out."

"I will. I promise," Molly said. "Why don't you give me your number?"

Derek gave it to her. She immediately texted him a smiley face. They went separate ways out of the coffee shop. Derek was eager to get away from the scene of all his interactions with Moss. *If he's not an agent, who is he? What does he want besides secret ingredients? He's got my number in his phone. If he's into illegal stuff, how far into it is he? Stovall must be in it too. The money in my bank account is real. I filled out a ton of paperwork at Stovall's office—address, date of birth, social security number, parent's name and address.* As he walked, he processed scenarios. He wasn't sure if he wanted to go home.

———

Derek didn't sleep well that first night. He was suspicious of every sound, inside and out. He felt violated. He was only glad he'd never shown Moss any outward signs of mistrust. Moss had no reason to think Derek would suspect he wasn't an agent. He thought about calling the police. He thought about calling the FBI. He thought about calling Mr. Bensen. But then he thought about the sinister grin. *What if he is somehow bad? If Stovall's in it with Moss—Stovall's an old colleague or investor or whatever. Maybe there is something going on and Mr. Bensen's involved and he's got me in the middle of it. I have no reason to think that's the case, but IF it is and I tell him what's going on, they could make the whole thing disappear before the government's able to do any real investigating.*

Derek decided it was best to let Molly do her job and let Caspian Sea pursue whatever they needed to pursue. He'd focus on learning what he could from Mr. Bensen. He slept a little better the next night, and a little better the night after that. Six days came and went—no calls or texts from Moss. No calls or texts from Molly either. Derek thought of texting her, but he didn't want to put pressure on her to act. The next Wednesday morning, he was in his 10:00 am class and Molly texted. "Gonna talk to Bloom. Fingers xd." He didn't reply. He didn't hear anything more from Molly for the rest of the day.

He didn't know what to expect when he walked off the elevator on the 23rd floor—crime scene tape from Mrs. Howe's desk across the entrance to the hallway? The doors opened and he stepped out into the office, which looked just the same as it always had.

"How are you?" Mrs. Howe asked with her usual smile.

"Good," Derek said. "You?"

"Just fine," she answered.

Derek walked down the hall and into the conference room and sat. Mr. Bensen soon joined him and sat down. He pulled Derek's folder over and opened it.

CHAPTER 9

CAPITAL BUDGETING II:
GROWING THE CORPORATE MONEY MACHINE

M r. Bensen looked over the work Derek had done since their last meeting. "Looks good. If I give you the cash flows of a project, then you can tell me IRR, right? And if I also give you the discount rate then you can tell me NPV, right?"

"Yes sir, sure can."

"My job is to maximize shareholder wealth. I'm always looking for projects to undertake that will increase shareholder value. The theory here is clean and simple. If the NPV is positive or the IRR is greater than k then I should do it. The value of Caspian Sea Drinks will increase by the same amount as the NPV of the project. My stockholders will be happy. I will have increased their wealth."

"Right," Derek said.

"Okay. That's theoretical. Let's take a step toward reality. I'm considering one such project right now. There's a new machine, the J-Mix 2000, that will mix the ingredients for Caspian Sea faster and allow us to bottle it more efficiently."

"Seriously?" Derek interrupted. "J-Mix 2000?"

"You into marketing or Finance? Who cares about the name? The engineers gave me a long, predictable pitch explaining how the J-Mix 2000 is so much better than what we're using now. They told me a bunch of technical details I don't care about."

"You only care about the cash flows, right? We don't care about the name—what the J stands for," Derek said, very animatedly. "We're not making a drink. We're running a money machine."

Mr. Bensen chuckled. "What's that? Your Bensen impression? Needs work. My CFO told me the machine costs $1 million and will increase cash flow by $320,000 for the next five years. Then the machine will be scrapped. He also said the discount rate is 9.78%. Should I buy it?"

Derek confidently attacked the calculator with the numbers and quickly said, "Yes. The NPV is $233,784.97 and the IRR is 18.03067%."

"Okay. Very precise. That's great in a Finance class, but out here on the Caspian Sea we're not that accurate. We're getting close to the end of these sessions so I'm going to let you in on a secret. Most of our numbers are guesses. I don't know that the discount rate should be exactly 9.34% and not 9.35%. I'm not sure that the future cash flows will be exactly $320,000 not $320,001. So I can't be sure that the NPV is exactly $233,784.97 and the IRR is 18.03067%.

"Don't get me wrong," Mr. Bensen said. "You have to get the math exactly right, but you also have to recognize when you *know* something versus when you are *estimating*. I know the J-Mix 2000 costs $1 million. The rest of the numbers are estimates. Now, I want to walk you through making those estimates."

"Cool," Derek said. He was still processing Mr. Bensen's acknowledgment that they were nearing the end of the sessions. He didn't know what that meant—if it was good or bad, but he didn't want to ask for clarification for fear of looking unsure of himself.

"Okay. First cost of capital, then cash flows," Mr. Bensen said. "The same principles for raising money—*capital*—apply to us today as they did when Alex and I got Stovall and Spencer to invest. We raise money by selling stocks or bonds. Our investors demand a return on their investment. That is our cost of capital. There is a cost for equity and a cost for debt. Combine the two and we have our overall cost of capital. We call it our WACC—*Weighted Average Cost of Capital*. The return we get on the project has to be greater than the cost of capital to fund the project.

"There are two ways to estimate the cost of equity and two ways to estimate the cost of debt. The good news is you've already done both. To estimate the cost of equity, k_e, we can use the CAPM or the constant growth version of the dividend discount model. To estimate the cost of debt, k_d, we can find the yield-to-maturity of our bonds or add a risk premium to the 10-year Treasury based on our credit rating." Mr. Bensen wrote on the board.

$$k_e = r_f + \beta[E(r_m) - r_f]$$

"Remember the CAPM? We can find the cost of equity if we know three things: the risk-free rate, Caspian Sea's β, and the market risk premium. We know all but three of them. And we don't even know that the CAPM is the appropriate model to use but we don't let lack of knowledge stop us. This is important. You have to know what the model is saying and what the weaknesses are. It's saying this: the return that investors require in order to buy Caspian Sea stock is the return they would get from investing in risk-free Treasury securities, plus a risk premium. That risk premium is equal to the market risk premium, $E(r_m) - r_f$, times a measure of Caspian Sea's relationship to the market, β.

"Assume r_f = 3.00%, the market risk premium is 6.00%, and that β equals 1.50. Do the math and you'll find our estimate for k_e is 12.00%.

"Let's try another approach that should get us to the same number. Remember that," Mr. Bensen wrote:

$$P_0 = \frac{D_1}{k_e - g}$$

"Rearrange and we have,

$$k_e = \frac{D_1}{P_0} + g$$

"I know that investors will pay $25.00 for our stock because that's the current market price," Mr. Bensen said. "Based on conversations with analysts who follow our stock, I'm pretty sure that they believe next year's dividend will be $2.00 and that the dividend will grow at 4.00% forever. Now let's do the math. You'll find that k_e equals 12.00%. Investors don't tell us directly what their required return is. Even if they did, words are empty. They tell us what they are willing to pay for the stock by actually purchasing it. We use the equation on the board to figure out their required rate of return. That's our cost of equity.

"We use the same logic to find our cost of debt. We know the payout rule for our debt. We know what the debt sells for. We know that the value of any financial asset is the present value of its expected future cash flows. Therefore, we can find the discount rate the market uses when valuing our debt. That is our cost of debt," Mr. Bensen said.

"For example, a recently issued Caspian Sea bond has a coupon rate of 5.00%, five years to maturity. Like almost all corporate bonds it has a par value of $1,000 and pays semi-annually. It sells for $990.00"

Derek went to work on the calculator. "The yield-to-maturity is 5.23%."

"Got it. The other way to estimate cost of debt is to look at our credit rating. If you go to a car lot to buy a car and want to finance it, they'll run your credit before they give you a loan. The higher your credit score, the lower your interest rate—your cost of debt. It's the same here. Suppose that the 10-year Treasury has a yield of 3.00% and that Caspian Sea has a BBB bond rating. The premium for BBB bonds is 2.23%. Our cost of debt is 3.00% plus 2.23% which is 5.23%.

"We need $1 million to buy the J-Mix 2000," Mr. Bensen continued. "We raise money by selling stocks and by selling bonds. Our cost of equity is 12.00% and our cost of debt is 5.23%. We need to know our cost of capital, which is the combined costs of equity and debt. The question is how do we combine the two costs?"

Derek didn't say anything.

"I'm asking," Mr. Bensen said.

"Yeah," Derek said. "I'm thinking." He paused another second looking at the board, "Wouldn't it depend on what percentage of your funding comes from equity and what percentage comes from debt? Say you raise $700,000 by selling stocks and $300,000 by selling bonds. Then Caspian Sea is 70% equity and 30% debt. So the cost of capital would be," Derek wrote:

$$0.70*.012 + .030*.0523$$

"Very close," Mr. Bensen said. First, it's the WACC. Second, debt has a tax advantage. Write the *Income Statement* on the board."

Derek looked at Mr. Bensen.

"A-ha! You weren't ready for that, huh? Take your time. Think about it."

Derek didn't grin. He wrote on the board.

	Sales
−	COGS
	Gross Profit
−	Operating Expenses
−	Depreciation
	Earnings before Interest and Taxes
−	Interest Expense
	Earnings before Taxes
−	Taxes
	Net Income

"A-ha!" Derek stepped away from the board. "See, I know this stuff. You subtract interest expense before you calculate taxes. The true cost of debt is not 5.23%. It's," Derek wrote on the board.

$$5.23\% * (1 - \text{tax rate})$$

"The average marginal tax rate for corporations in the U.S. is about 40%," Derek continued. "Then the WACC must be," he wrote on the board.

$$WACC = w_e k_e + w_d k_d (1 - \tau)$$

$$= 0.70 * 0.12 + 0.30 * 0.0523 * (1 - 0.40) = 0.0934$$

"That's why your CFO said the cost of capital was 9.34%. And that's why the number is an estimate and not the truth," Derek said.

"Nice," Mr. Bensen said looking at the board, nodding.

"And that's why I should be your CFO," said Derek and crossed his arms and nodded and grinned.

"Slow down there cowboy," Mr. Bensen said. "Next let's talk cash flows. We're looking for what's called *Incremental Cash Flows*. I want to know what cash flows Caspian Sea would have if we did the project and what cash flows we would have if we didn't do the project. The difference is the incremental cash flows. I use those to make my decision. The decision to buy or not to buy the J-Mix 2000 is a good example of a relatively simple project. Most will follow the same pattern we have here. We'll add some twists in a few minutes.

"We have an initial cash outflow," Mr. Bensen said "the cost of the machine—"

"$1 million," Derek interrupted.

Mr. Bensen continued. "Then we estimate operating cash flows of $320,000 for years 1 through 5. Think about where that estimate came from. The J-Mix 2000 will make more product so we'll have more revenues. But it will cost money to hire people to operate it and money to pay for the electricity it takes to run it. In other words, it will increase our operating expenses. If we're making more money then we'll have to pay more taxes."

"Let me take a shot at this," Derek said. "Back to the *Income Statement*, right? How much will sales increase?"

"$500,000. And good question. It's not *what will sales be?* It's *how much will sales increase* because of the J-Mix 2000?"

"What will the change in COGS and operating costs be?" Derek asked.

"$100,000 total. No need to distinguish between COGS and operating expenses."

"Depreciation?" Derek asked.

"You tell me," Mr. Bensen said. "In five years the machine'll be worn out."

"In Accounting we learned several different ways to do depreciation," Derek said.

"Let's keep it simple," Mr. Bensen replied, "and use a straight line and assume the machine will be depreciated to a value of zero over its life of five years."

"Then depreciation is $1 million divided by 5. $200,000." Derek wrote on the board.

$$\text{Incremental Cash Flow} = [\text{Revenue} - \text{Costs} - \text{Depreciation}]$$
$$(1 - \text{tax rate}) + \text{Depreciation}$$

"Right," Mr. Bensen said. "Why did you add back depreciation and why did you use *Revenues* instead of *Sales*?"

"Depreciation is not a cash flow," Derek answered. "Revenues and Sales mean the same thing."

"Work through the numbers. Show me what you mean."

Derek wrote on the board.

$$500,000 - 100,000 = 400,000$$

"The J-Mix 2000 increases my profit by \$400,000 but I have to pay taxes," Derek said. "My taxes are not \$400,000 times 40%. I get to deduct depreciation. My taxes are:

$$(500,000 - 100,000 - 200,000)*0.40 = 80,000$$

"So the increase in operating cash flow is:

$$400,000 - 80,000 = 320,000$$

"The equation I wrote on the board is just a shortcut," Derek said.

"I'm impressed," Mr. Bensen said. "You have a pretty good handle on this capital budgeting thing. This week's assignment is very important. There are some twists that we didn't talk about. I made some notes. Work through the problems carefully."

STUDY PACKET: PROJECTS

Mutually Exclusive Projects with Equal Lives

Caspian Sea Drinks owns an undeveloped parcel of land that is ideally located to construct a new bottling facility. The engineers at Caspian Sea Drinks have two proposals for the facility. One design, call it Project A, costs more to build while the other, call it Project B, is more expensive to operate. The engineering department was unable to clearly articulate why that is the case. The projects are called *mutually exclusive* because the Caspian Sea may do either project but not both. They may do neither one of the projects and keep the land, or they may sell the land at the market price. To make his decision Mr. Bensen and his team will identify the incremental cash flows of each project, estimate his cost of capital, and then calculate the NPV and IRR of each project.

The CFO of Caspian Sea Drinks believes the incremental cash flows of the two projects are as follows. Project A will have an initial cash flow of -$50 million and incremental cash flows of $5,445,000 million for years 1–20. Project B will have an initial cash flow of –$37 million and incremental cash flows of $3,960,000 million for years 1–20. The CFO estimates CSD's WACC to be 8.50%.

What are the NPV and IRR of each project using the CFO's estimates? Which project should be done? Why?

Answer. NPV_A = $1,527,867.83, IRR_A = 8.917%; NPV_B = $474,812.97, IRR_B = 8.676%. Choose Project A because it has a higher NPV.

Estimating incremental cash flows

Mr. Bensen decides to verify the CFO's estimates by creating his own estimates from raw the data. His research shows the following.

Caspian Sea paid $1.5 million for the lot in 2008. If the lot were sold CSD would receive $3 million after all real estate taxes and fees.[1] Site prep work necessary before constructing either facility has been done at a cost of $50,000. An outside design firm has done some preliminary work for each project. The work for Project A cost $20,000 and the work for Project B cost $25,000. The cost of constructing and equipping the Project A design is $50 million while the cost of constructing and equipping the Project B design is $37 million. He discovers that Project A will require an initial increase in net working capital of $1 million while Project B will require an initial increase in net working capital of $2 million.[2] The working capital will return to pre-project levels at the end of the life of each project.

Mr. Bensen knows not to consider *sunk costs*. Sunk costs are any costs which have already been paid or costs for which Caspian Sea Drinks has already committed payment. The decision to accept or reject the project depends solely on how the cash flows will be different if the project is or is not accepted—the *incremental cash flows*. The payment of sunk costs does not depend on the decision to accept or reject the project.

He also knows to include *opportunity costs*. Opportunity costs are benefits not received because the project was accepted. If Caspian Sea rejects the project they can sell the land. Effectively foregoing the sale of the land is a cost.

The initial cash flow for Project A is:

---

1 For compositional ease the term 'market value' will mean the amount a company would receive for selling land after all taxes and fees are paid. The firm must estimate the value of the land at the conclusion of the project. Assume the firm may sell the land for this value. For simplicity, assume the firm must pay income tax on this amount.
2 Net working capital is current assets minus current liabilities. An increase is effectively a negative cash flow and a decrease is a positive cash flow. This is included to capture true cash flows and not just accounting earnings. For example, accounts receivable may increase because more sales are on credit.

$CF0_A = -\$50 \text{ million} - \$3 \text{ million} - \$1 \text{ million} = -\$54 \text{ million}.$

The initial cash flow for Project B is:

$CF0_B = -\$37 \text{ million} - \$3 \text{ million} - \$2 \text{ million} = -\$42 \text{ million}.$

Mr. Bensen realizes that the CFO forgot to adjust the incremental cash flows for depreciation. He calculates then from scratch. For Project A, revenues are expected to be \$16,500,000 per year for 20 years. Costs are expected to be 45% of revenues. The plant and equipment is depreciated on a straight line basis for 20 years to a book value of \$3,000,000.[3] For Project B, revenues are expected to be \$16,500,000 per year for 20 years. Costs are expected to be 60% of revenues. The plant and equipment is depreciated on a straight line basis for 20 years to a book value of \$3,000,000. Caspian Sea Drinks has a marginal tax rate of 40%.

The incremental cash flows for Project A are:

$$OCF_A = (16,500,000 - 7,425,000 - 2,350,000)(1-0.40) + 2,350,000 = 6,385,000$$

The incremental cash flows for Project B are:

$$OCF_B = (16,500,000 - 9,900,000 - 1,700,000)(1-0.40) + 1,700,000 = 4,640,000$$

In the final year of both projects the plant and equipment is sold for its book value[4] and the net working capital returns to pre-project

---

3 Depreciation equals (Cost of plant and equipment – book value)/number of years of economic life. Land is not depreciated.
4 If the equipment is sold for more than its book value then the firm must pay capital gains tax. If it is sold for less the firm has a taxable loss. For simplicity, assume that capital gains tax rates are the same as the firm's

levels. The land is estimated to have a market value of $5 million at the completion of the project. Therefore, the total cash flow in year 20 for Project A is:

$$\$6,385,000 + \$3,000,000 + \$1,000,000 + 5,000,000 =$$
$$\$15,385,000.$$

The total cash flow in year 20 for Project B is:

$$\$4,640,000 + \$3,000,000 + \$2,000,000 + 5,000,000 =$$
$$\$14,640,000.$$

Calculate the NPV and IRR of each project with the updated estimates for the cash flows. Which project do you accept? Why?

Answer. $NPV_A = \$8,183,951.73$, $IRR_A = 10.440\%$; $NPV_B = \$3,866,045.74$, $IRR_B = 9.666\%$. Choose Project A because it has a higher NPV.

If the marginal tax rate was 45% how would the NPV of each project change? How might the corporate tax rate affect the economy as a whole?

Answer. It would lower the NPV of each project. Without knowing the cost of debt in the WACC calculation it is impossible to know by how much. Higher corporate tax rates will cause some projects that had a positive NPV to become negative NPV projects.

---

margin tax rate in income. Further assume that the firm uses any capital loss on a particular project to offset a capital gain on another.

Mutually Exclusive Projects with unequal lives

Engineering alerts Mr. Bensen that the estimate for the life of Project B was wrong. It will only have a life of 18 years. Updated cash flow projections show that Project A will have an initial cost of $54 million and produce incremental cash flows of $6 million each year for 20 years. They also show that Project B will have an initial cost of $42 million and produce incremental cash flows of $5 million each year for 18 years. The projects may be repeated indefinitely.

Since the projects have unequal lives one cannot choose between them by simply looking at the NPV. Rather one must estimate the *equivalent annual series*. Caspian Sea Drinks is indifferent between executing the project and receiving an immediate payment equal to the NPV of the project. The equivalent annual series is the annual payment over the life of the project that would be of the same value as the immediate payment of the NPV. If both projects can be repeated indefinitely then Caspian Sea Drinks should choose the project with the most attractive equivalent annual series. Find the equivalent annual series for each project. Which one should they choose?

The NPV of Project A is $2,780,019.85. Therefore, Caspian Sea Drinks is indifferent between executing the project and receiving a one-time payment of $2,780,019.85 today. Receiving $2,780,019.85 today is equivalent to receiving $293,767.38 per year for 20 years. In the financial calculator:

$$n = 20$$
$$PV = 2,780,019.85$$
$$FV = 0$$
$$I/y = 8.50$$

Solving for *pmt* results in $293,767.38.

The NPV of Project B is $3,277,382.19. Therefore, Caspian Sea Drinks is indifferent between executing the project and receiving a one-time payment of $3,277,382.19 today. Receiving $3,277,382.19 today is equivalent to receiving $361,922.67 per year for 18 years. In the financial calculator:

$$n = 18$$
$$PV = 3,277,382.19$$
$$FV = 0$$
$$I/y = 8.50$$

Solving for *pmt* results in $361,922.67.

Mr. Bensen will select Project B because it will create the equivalent of an infinite cash flow stream of $361,922.67 per year forever.

Product Cannibalization

Caspian Sea Drinks is considering the production of a new beverage based on pomegranates. The project will have an initial cost of $20 million and have a 20 year life. Marketing estimates that total revenues generated by the sale of the new drink are estimated to be $10 million. Costs are estimated to be $6.5 million. The marginal tax rate is 40% and the WACC is 10.0%. Find the NPV.

Incremental cash flows = (10 mm – 6.5 mm – 1 mm)*(1– 0.40) + 1 mm = 2.5 mm

$$NPV = \$1,283,909.30$$

Mr. Bensen realizes that the estimates are for total revenues and costs. Ten percent of the sales of the new pomegranate drink will come from existing Caspian Sea Drinks customers who switch from the plum-based drink. Therefore, revenues and costs should be reduced by 10%. So,

Incremental cash flows = (9 mm – 5.85 mm – 1 mm)*(1–
0.40) + 1 mm = 2.29 mm

NPV = -$503,939.08.

PROBLEM SET

1. Caspian Sea Drinks is considering the purchase of a new water filtration system produced by Rube Goldberg Machines. This new equipment, the RGM-7000, will allow Caspian Sea Drinks to expand production. Mr. Bensen gave Derek the following information. Use it to estimate the incremental cash flows for produced by the RGM-7000. Then find the IRR.
   a. The RGM-7000 will cost $12,000,000 fully installed. It will be fully depreciated over a 15 year life, then removed for no cost.
   b. The PJX5 will increase revenues by $2,600,000 per year and reduce operating costs by $500,000 per year.
   c. CSD's marginal tax rate is 40%.
2. Use the following to estimate CSD's WACC.
   a. CSD's capital structure is 65% equity and 35% debt.
   b. CSD's 10-year, semi-annual pay, 5.00% coupon bond sells for $990 or 99% of par.
   c. CSD's stock currently has a market value of $25.00 and Mr. Bensen believes the market estimates that dividends will grow at 5.00% forever. Next year's dividend is projected to be $2.00.
3. Use information in #1 and #2 to find the NPV of the RGM-7000 purchase. Should Mr. Bensen approve the purchase? How will his decision affect the value of CSD? If CSD's tax rate is raised to 45% will Mr. Bensen make the same decision?

4. Caspian Sea Drinks is considering the purchase of a plum juicer—the PJX5. There is no planned increase in production. The PJX5 will reduce costs by squeezing more juice from each plum and doing so in a more efficient manner. Mr. Bensen gave Derek the following information. Use it to determine if CSD should purchase the PJX5.
   a. The PJX5 will cost $2,000,000 fully installed and has a 10 year life. It will be depreciated to a book value of $100,000 and sold for that amount in year 10.
   b. The Engineering Department spent $10,000 researching the various juicers.
   c. Portions of the plant floor have been redesigned to accommodate the juicer at a cost of $17,000.
   d. The PJX5 will reduce operating costs by $400,000 per year.
   e. CSD's marginal tax rate is 35%.
   f. CSD's capital structure is 70% equity and 30% debt.
   g. CSD's 10-year, semi-annual pay, 5.00% coupon bond sells for $1,010 or 101% of par.
   h. CSD's stock currently has a market value of $20.00 and Mr. Bensen believes the market estimates that dividends will grow at 4.00% forever. Next year's dividend is projected to be $1.50.
5. Caspian Sea Drinks is considering the production of a diet drink. The expansion of the plant and the purchase of the equipment necessary to produce the diet drink will cost $25 million. The plant and equipment will be depreciated over 10 years to a book value of $2 million. Net working capital will increase by $1 million at the beginning of the project and will be recovered at the end. The new diet drink will produce revenues of $8,000,000 per year and cost $2,000,000 per year over the 10-year life of the project. Marketing estimates 10% of the buyers of the diet drink will be people who will switch from the regular drink. The

marginal tax rate is 40%. The WACC is 12%. Find the NPV and IRR.

6. Assume the Caspian Sea Drinks CFO forgot to adjust his cash flow estimates in #5 for product cannibalization. How would that change his NPV and IRR estimates?

7. HM, Inc. is considering building a plant on land they bought two years ago for $500,000. Use the following information to find the NPV and IRR of the project.

   a. The expansion will require the purchase of machinery costing $40,000,000.

   b. The market value of the land is $750,000. The estimated value of the land 20 years from today is $2,000,000.

   c. The firm has spent $250,000 to train workers to use the new machinery.

   d. The sales from this project will be $15 million per year, of which 5% comes from lost sales of existing products. Costs will be $7,000,000.

   e. The company uses straight-line depreciation. The project has an economic life of 20 years and the machinery will a book value of $4,000,000.

   f. Because of the project, the company will need additional working capital of $1,500,000 which can be liquidated at the end of 20 years.

   g. HM's stock price is $34.50. They just paid a dividend of $3 and the market consensus is for constant 5% dividend growth forever.

   h. HM's bonds sell for $970. They pay semi-annually, have 7 years to maturity, a coupon rate of 4% and par value of $1,000.

   i. HM's marginal tax rate is 40%.

   j. Their target capital structure is 70% equity and 30% debt.

8. Godbey Motor Works is the world's premiere car manufacturer. They are considering buying a new piece of equipment, the

AEG7, to make the production of the Escalate more efficient. The AEG7 will allow GMW to produce cars faster while reducing energy use and repairs. The AEG7 costs $10 million, will increase revenue by $2.5 million per year and reduce costs by $600,000 per year. The economic life of the AEG7 is 10 years after which it will be sold for a book value of $1,000,000. GMW's marginal tax rate is 40%.

Estimate the cash flows for the project.

GMW has an AA rating and the risk-free rate is 3.00%.

Rating	Default premium
AAA	1.50%
AA	2.00%
A	2.50%
BBB	3.00%
BB	5.00%

GMW's bonds sell for $984.41, have a par value is $1,000, 10 years to maturity, a coupon rate is 4.800%, and pay semi-annually.

The riskless rate is 3%, the market risk premium is 6% and GMW's β is 1.50. GMW's stock sells for $25.00. It is expected to pay a dividend of $2.00 next year and the dividend is expected to grow at 4% forever.

GMW is 60% equity and 40% debt. Estimate GMW's WACC. Verify that, in this case, the two methods for estimating cost of debt and the two methods for estimating cost of equity give the same results.

Find the NPV and IRR for this project.

9. A firm is considering replacing the existing industrial air conditioning unit. They will pick one of two units. The first, the AC360, costs $25,000 to install, $5,000 to operate per year for 7 years at which time it will be sold for $7,000. The second, RayCool 8, costs $40,000 to install, $2,000 to operate per year for 7 years at which time it will be sold for $9,000. The firm's cost of capital is 5%. Which unit should they buy?

10. Repeat #9 but assume the AC360 only has a 5-year life. What is the equivalent annual cost of the best project?

11. A firm is must choose to buy the GSU-3300 or the UGA-3000. Both machines make the firm's production process more efficient which in turn increases incremental cash flows. The GSU-3300 produces incremental cash flows of $25,000 per year for 8 years and costs $100,000. The UGA-3000 produces incremental cash flows of $27,000 per year for 9 years and cost $125,000. The firm's WACC is 7%. Which machine should they buy? Why?

12. Estimate the incremental cash flows for the following project. Then find the IRR and NPV assuming a 10% WACC.

   a. The equipment cost $12,000,000 installed and is fully depreciated over its 8-year economic life.

   b. Costs will be reduced by $3,250,000 per year for the 8 years of the project. Revenues will be unchanged.

   c. The equipment is sold for $1,000,000 at the completion of the project.

13. Repeat #12 assuming the equipment is sold for $3,000,000 at the end of the project.

9.1

Mr. Bensen and Derek both got up from their chairs. "So we're getting near the end?" Derek asked. He wondered if Mr. Bensen had heard anything from Bloom, if Molly had even talked to Bloom.

"Yeah, I think so," Mr. Bensen stretched. "As far as I can tell you're getting this stuff, and I've gotta be honest, I'm kind of drying up. I mean there's more to talk about, but I'm not sure what direction it should take. Depending on how you do with this stuff, I think next week might be our last session."

Derek didn't say anything.

"What?" Mr. Bensen chuckled. "Don't get all sad on me. You dig this all that much?"

Derek shrugged and chuckled, "I'm not sad. I'm kind of a routine kind of guy. I'm all in the routine of coming here once a week—I'll have to adjust, that's all."

"You'll be fine," Mr. Bensen patted Derek on the back as they turned to walk out of the room. For the first time, Mr. Bensen went left out of the conference room instead of turning right and going back to his office. Derek stopped in the hallway, wondering. Mr. Bensen turned around as he walked and looked at Derek standing still. He waved back at him, "Get outta here, you'll be fine. Next week."

Derek waved and walked to the elevators. *He's walking down there. He's never gone that way before. I bet Molly talked to Bloom. Maybe they've got the crime scene tape down there, around all of Research and Development. Maybe that's why Molly hasn't texted again. She's stuck in with investigators and agents and police, showing her photos of Moss, asking questions. She's probably terrified. Probably got them all thinking she wants to ask them to the prom. This is gonna come back to me at some point. Sooner than later. I should've told Mr. Bensen.*

Derek walked out of the building, still thinking. He had his phone out, debating whether or not to text Molly. *If they're all up there with her, they've got her phone. She'll get the text from me and they'll triangulate the signal and they'll swarm me right here. It's a good thing I didn't text her back from class.*

"Derek!" said a big voice from directly behind his head. As soon as he heard his name he was engulfed by a huge and heavy arm around his shoulder and a hand gripping his right arm from behind. He was in a walking hug with Stovall who kept talking excitedly, "Buddy! It's been a while! How you been? How's everything?"

Derek was sure it was Stovall—he remembered the size and the voice—but he was trying to get a look at him as Stovall steered him down the sidewalk. Stovall was wearing jeans and a long-sleeved T-shirt, a baseball hat, and shades. He leaned on Derek so he couldn't turn his head and whispered through his smile, "Don't look at me. Walk to the park. You're gonna tell me what's going on and where Toth is." Stovall let go of Derek and walked a bit behind him as they headed to the park. Derek tried to remember what he'd heard about Stovall from Moss and what he'd heard about him from Mr. Bensen. *Toth. Stovall talked about Toth the first time they met. Moss never said who Toth was. At least we're going to the park. He's not crazy enough to do anything terrible with people around—kneecap my head or anything.* He remembered Moss saying something about Stovall being on some sort of medication. *What if he ran out?* Derek gulped. He walked into the park like he had so many other times. He looked up the walkway at the bench. For the first time, someone else was sitting there—a man in a suit and sunglasses, folded paper in one hand, cup of coffee in another. Derek stopped.

"What's the problem?" Stovall asked.

"That's where we always sit—where I always sit," Derek said.

"Keep walking, there's other benches."

Derek kept walking and Stovall followed. Derek looked for another empty bench further in the park. They walked by the man with the newspaper and coffee.

"Where you boys off to?"

Derek and Stovall both stopped and turned around to look down at the man, who took a sip from his coffee cup.

"Isn't this your spot?" the man asked, looking at Derek.

Derek and Stovall said nothing.

"Sit down," the man said. "There's room."

"Let's go," Stovall said to Derek and pointed up the path. They both took a few steps.

"Mr. Stovall, are you looking for Billy Toth?" the man asked.

Derek stopped. Stovall turned around quickly, angry, and launched over at the bench. "Where is he?"

The man on the bench put down his paper and stood up and opened his jacket slightly to reveal a badge and a holstered gun. Derek felt his entire body relax.

"Whoa," said Stovall. "What's all this?"

Derek, suddenly exhausted, walked over and slumped down into his usual spot on the bench while the two men stood staring at each other.

"I'm looking for my accountant," Stovall said. "This young man's been meeting with him regularly. I thought he might know his whereabouts. Why is this your concern?"

"Special Agent Brown, FBI," the man said and offered his hand to Stovall. Stovall shook it. "Your accountant, otherwise known as Special Agent Moss, is in some trouble." Derek sat and shook his head. "Derek, I know you like this spot, but I think we'd all be a little more comfortable back upstairs in the conference room."

"How do you know me?" Derek asked.

"Let's go up to Caspian Sea and we'll all get to sit and swap some stories. Maybe have a drink. Mr. Stovall, feel free to call your lawyer."

Derek led the way from the park up to the Caspian Sea conference room. Inside the room, his seat was taken again—many of the seats were taken. Derek recognized Mr. Bensen and Molly and two other men. He assumed one of the men was Dr. Bloom and the other was a Caspian Sea lawyer. Across the table from Mr. Bensen, in Derek's usual seat, with his back to the door, sat Moss/Toth. The two seats next to him were empty. Agent Brown motioned for Stovall and Derek to sit in those.

Apparently, Moss/Toth had been in the building while Derek and Mr. Bensen were in their meeting. He came to the office to see Molly and talk to her more about the secret ingredients and about taking a trip to the Caspian Sea. Molly, very nervous upon looking up from her desk and seeing Moss, went into her flirtation mode, which led to her taking Moss for a walk around the office. As the two walked, they ran into Dr. Bloom. Molly introduced Moss to Dr. Bloom as "the nice man I told you about earlier." Molly and Moss continued their walk, while Dr. Bloom called the authorities, the corporate lawyer, and tried to reach Mr. Bensen. Mrs. Howe knew Mr. Bensen didn't like to be disturbed when in meetings, and she knew he'd be finished with Derek soon. A handful of agents were in the Caspian Sea offices within minutes of Dr. Bloom's phone call. They found Molly and Moss/Toth and arrested him quickly for impersonating a government agent. Toth denied any criminal activity and said only that he was working for Sean Stovall and wanted his lawyer. Normal procedure would have called for Toth to be taken in immediately for questioning and processing. However, an agent on the street had recognized Stovall lurking around outside and was about to arrest him but was told to try to bring him in discreetly. This was about the time Derek walked out of the building and was approached by Stovall. The agent, who had been assigned to Toth for weeks, knew Toth often met Derek in the park. He called his partner, agent Brown, and Brown met Stovall and Derek at the bench.

After a few words of apology from the ranking agent to Mr. Bensen, all the agents cleared out of the room with Stovall and Toth. Toth was in handcuffs.

Derek didn't know what to say. He looked across the table at Mr. Bensen and Molly. Molly smiled and said, "Hey."

Mr. Bensen asked, "Who's up for pizza?"

Two hours later, the pizza boxes were empty and every question asked had been answered. Things were tense in the beginning, though no accusations were ever leveled, but they relaxed in the end. Molly's explanation of the nephew situation bothered Mr. Bensen initially, but Dr. Bloom assured him he'd taken appropriate measures and they ended up having several laughs about what other appropriate measures could be taken against the bullies to avenge Molly. Derek even had an opportunity to apologize for lying about his fear of crowded elevators.

At about 6:30 pm, Mr. Bensen said, "Let's go home. Dr. Bloom, thanks for hanging out with us and taking care of Molly. Molly, thanks for doing your job and telling the truth. Derek, thanks for bringing an almost perfect storm to Caspian Sea." He laughed.

"I'm sorry," Derek said, smiling. "I don't know what to say."

"Go home," Mr. Bensen said and patted him on the back. "Do your homework."

—

Derek had a pleasantly uneventful week. He was a little anxious before going into Caspian Sea for the last time, but he felt great knowing there was nothing to hide and nothing to think about other than showing Mr. Bensen his investment was worth it.

When Mrs. Howe greeted him he didn't sense any awareness that this was his final visit, so he proceeded like it was any other Wednesday and walked down to the conference room. The door was closed. Mr. Bensen was standing at the window, arms crossed, looking out toward the neighboring buildings. He looked deep in thought. Derek didn't want to disturb him. He also didn't want to chance another sinister grin. He opened the door.

"Hey! Quick, come here!" Mr. Bensen said.

Derek was confused. He paused to look at a Chick-Fil-A bag on the table, then walked over to the window.

"C'mon! Quick! Quick! Aww! Ha!" Mr. Bensen unfolded his arms and laughed hard, but kept looking out the window. Derek got to the window and looked out for something funny. "You missed it! See that dude down there? Right there, in the red sweat pants."

"Holding his hat?"

"Yeah. He's a genius. I don't know if he's moves all over town or what, but I've seen him right there a few times. You see those bushes over there—Wait! He's going in again. Okay, watch."

Mr. Bensen folded his arms again. He and Derek watched the man who'd been holding his hat, put it back on and squat behind a short row of hedge that lined the front of a building on a corner across the street. Derek looked at Mr. Bensen, puzzled. Mr. Bensen, with a sinister grin, just pointed down and said, "Watch!" The man watched a few people walk by, then sprang out at a couple walking holding hands. The girlfriend grabbed her face and screamed, though they couldn't hear the scream up in the conference room. The boyfriend jumped back and into some kind of martial-arts crouch and then fell down. Mr. Bensen and Derek both exploded in laughter.

"Unbelievable!" Derek said.

"No, this is the best part! Watch!"

Derek looked back down. The boyfriend, clearly laughing, was pulling out his wallet. He pulled out a few bills, dropped them in the man's hat, which he had removed and was humbly holding out. The man nodded in thanks to the boyfriend. The boyfriend slapped him on the back, put his arm around his girlfriend, and the couple walked away smiling and laughing.

"Brilliant. That's it, Derek. There's the next guest speaker for your Finance Club. That guy's a genius."

They both dropped into their seats, smiling, and shaking their heads.

CHAPTER 10

SPECIAL TOPICS AND UNANSWERED QUESTIONS: FINE TUNING THE MACHINE

I loved the last day of elementary school," said Mr. Bensen as they entered the conference room. He put a Chick-fil-A milkshake on the table in front of Derek. Derek grinned. "The last day of school was really the day *before* the last because the last day was chocolate cupcakes and 2-liters of root beer and Coke."

"The school gave you Coke?" Derek asked. "Man, all we got was celery sticks and peanut butter and sugar-free lemonade."

"Cheers," Mr. Bensen said, raising his milkshake.

"Amen," said Derek.

"Okay. Before we get all sentimental, this is not like elementary school. We've still got work to do on the last day," Mr. Bensen said, "but it's still gonna be fun. I wanna hit several topics in no particular order—the fun stuff in Finance. First, the most fun of all—going public.

"Caspian Sea Drinks was a privately held corporation. By law we were limited to 499 shareholders. We had huge growth potential."

"Lots of NPV-positive projects," Derek said.

"Yeah. And we needed money," Mr. Bensen said. "Alex, Spencer, and I had put in all we could. The angel investors put in all they could and the venture capitalists put in all they wanted to. Those guys, mainly the venture capitalists, wanted to cash out. I wanted cash too. On paper I was rich but I didn't have money. I had shares in Caspian Sea Drinks. Going public would do all that. It would let the venture capitalists cash out, let me get in a position to sell some shares, and raise capital for all these great NPV-positive projects.

"Going public is a complex process. I know how to run Caspian Sea Drinks. I know my company. I know how to manage the people, how to market the brand, and how to make the money machine run efficiently. But the rules and regulations of going public are overwhelming. I can't explain every detail, but I'll walk you through a brief overview of what we did," Mr. Bensen said.

"First, we called in investment bankers from JPMorgan Chase. Again, Caspian Sea was a money machine. The first step is to value the money machine."

"Size, timing, risk," Derek said.

Mr. Bensen continued, "The investment banker looked at the size, timing, and risk of our cash flows and came up with a value. Notice I said *a value* not *the value*. Like you, they know the mathematical equations to find the value. They don't know the size, timing, and risk of the future cash flows. They can only estimate them. So the result of their calculations is an estimate of the value of Caspian Sea Drinks. I sat down with the bankers and my CFO and some of my other top people and talked through the estimates. That took forever, and it was exhausting. But it worked.

"Now that the investment bankers have some belief about the value of Caspian Sea they do a *road show*. These guys have taken many companies public in the past and will take many public in the future. They know investors who will be interested not only in IPOs but in an IPO by a company like Caspian Sea. The road show is an infomercial about why you should buy shares of Caspian Sea. Among other things, the bankers will tell potential investors what percent of the company is for sale and how much they expect each share to cost. They then ask for orders."

"Orders?" Derek asked.

"Yeah. Think of the company as a pie. I'll show you the pie and tell you how good it tastes. Then I'll say we're going to sell slices and here's how big the slice is. Now you tell me how many slices you want and how much you will pay. At this point you're not obligated to buy. The road show is just to gauge interest. You can smell the pie but you can't taste it," Mr. Bensen said.

"Assume you're a sophisticated pie eater—an investor. You're invited by JPMorgan Chase to the road show. You've been to these infomercials put on by JPMorgan Chase before and bought some pie—some shares. Why do you come to the road show for Caspian Sea?"

"Because I liked the last pie the JPMorgan Chase people sold me," Derek replied.

"Exactly," Mr. Bensen said. "You can learn a lot about Caspian Sea. You can do your homework, but you'll never know as much about the company as I do or as much about the true value of the company and the investment bankers. That's called *Information Asymmetry*. You buy Caspian Sea in large part based on trust in the investment bankers. That's called *Reputational Capital*. Reputational capital is extremely valuable to investment bankers. If you feel they didn't treat you fairly, then you won't be back. Neither will your friends.

"JPMorgan Chase will put together a syndicate of other investment banking firms. As a group they will buy all the shares to be issued directly from Caspian Sea Drinks. Then they'll try to sell the shares to investors from the road show for 7% more or $21.40. Suppose you buy 10,000 shares from the syndicate at $21.40 per share. You write a check for $214,000.00. What do you want to happen now?" Mr. Bensen asked.

"I want the share price to go up."

"Obviously, right? If the share price goes to $32.10 by market close at 4:00 pm that day, you'd be pretty happy. Your $214,000 investment is now worth $321,000. That's a 50% return in one day. The investment banker just made your list of favorite people. But what about me? Am I happy?" Mr. Bensen asked.

"Yeah," Derek answered. "The value of your shares went up 50% too."

"Nope. You missed that one," Mr. Bensen said. "I didn't buy at $21.40. My share of Caspian Sea would have the same value if the price at the beginning of the day was $32.10. I'm not happy because Caspian Sea lost a bunch of money. The bankers could have paid Caspian Sea $30.00 per share and sold for 7% more or $32.10. If there were buyers willing to pay $32.10 at 4:00 pm, there must have been buyers willing to pay the same amount at 9:30 am.

"The bankers told us that Caspian Sea Drinks was worth $1.2 billion. That means we could have 60 million shares worth $20 each. We could've had 120 million shares worth $10 each. Every Thanksgiving my wife cuts the pumpkin pie into really small slices hoping that I'll eat less pie. Doesn't work. I just eat more pieces. If you cut Caspian Sea into more shares it doesn't matter. My $20 will buy more shares.

"Back to the point," Mr. Bensen said. "Caspian Sea sold 20% of the 60 million shares. That's 12 million shares. At $20 per share, Caspian Sea had $240 million to use to create more wealth, to undertake positive-NPV projects. That's great but we could've sold the 12 million shares for $30 each. That's $360 million to feed into the money machine to make more money. We left $120 million on the table," Mr. Bensen said.

"So this is real? This happened?" Derek asked. "Did you fire them? Sue them?"

"Yes it's real," Mr. Bensen grinned. "I thanked them. The bankers need to keep potential investors happy by pricing IPOs so that they go up in value. They need to keep CEOs like me happy by getting a sufficiently high price for the shares. That puts them in a tight spot. There are some interesting and unanswered questions here. Exactly how much money should be left on the table? How can the bankers find a better estimate of true value? Should Caspian Sea Drinks have gone public in the first place? Why does the government limit the number of investors in a private company to 499? Should the government require more or less financial regulation of publicly traded corporations?

"But here's what we know: after the IPO we were wildly successful. We were growing fast and Coca-Cola noticed. They didn't have a plum-flavored drink and people were going crazy for it. Coke had a choice. They could develop their own plum drink or buy us. How should they decide?"

"Is it an NPV project?" Derek thought aloud. "They should do the analysis to see if developing a plum drink would be a positive-NPV project—same for buying Caspian Sea. If both are positive-NPV projects then they should do the one with the highest NPV. They've gotta maximize shareholder wealth."

"Correct, but easier said than done." Mr. Bensen pointed out. "Coke did the analysis and decided to acquire us. They hired investment bankers and made us an offer. We hired investment bankers to advise us about their offer. My job is to maximize shareholder wealth. I have three choices: accept the offer, seek another offer, or determine that Caspian Sea Drinks will be more valuable as a stand-alone company and reject the offer. I have a fourth choice. I love running Caspian Sea Drinks. It's why I get up in the morning. I built it from nothing. I've made many people rich. Caspian Sea Drinks will never be sold to anyone for any price. Who cares about maximizing shareholder wealth? This is my company.

"Ethically, I couldn't take that fourth option. I take my charge to maximize shareholder wealth seriously. Some CEOs don't, which raises an interesting question. Remember how corporations are structured? Shareholders elect a board of directors. The board hires and fires management. Theoretically, if I don't do the right thing—as defined by the board—then the board will fire me and get a CEO who will. But boards are people, not robots. What makes a good board? Who should be on it? What should their backgrounds be? What should their incentives be? How many people should be on the board?

"If I'm not acting in the best interest of the shareholders and the board isn't either, what can be done?" Mr. Bensen continued. "The shareholders can vote in a new board. But how? When? Can the whole board be replaced at the annual shareholders meeting or only a few of them? If you only own 1,000 shares out of 60 million shares, is it worth it for you to come to the meeting? Do any of the individual shareholders have a sufficient incentive to be active in forcing change?

"Coke did make an offer. We negotiated and came to a deal. I thought it was a good deal for my shareholders. The Coke CEO thought it was a good deal for his. Neither of us knew for sure. We announced the deal and shares of both companies went up in value. That told us that other investors thought it was a good deal too.

"Coke offered cash and shares. In other words, each Caspian Sea shareholder got some cash and some shares of Coke. Caspian Sea Drinks was now owned by Coca-Cola. We kept the name for marketing purposes. They wanted my team and me to stay on and run Caspian Sea. I was happy too. The deal worked because of synergies. That means two plus two equals five."

"Radiohead," Derek interrupted.

"Huh?"

"2 + 2 = 5. It's a song title," Derek explained. "Sorry, you were on a roll."

"That might be the only place Radiohead and Corporate Finance intersect," Mr. Bensen said. "Fake Plastic Money Machines." Derek chuckled, impressed with Mr. Bensen's awareness. "So, synergy. Coke and I realized that, together, we could do more and do it more efficiently than we could as separate companies.

"The question is *why?*" Mr. Bensen said. "*Why did we have synergies? Why do some mergers and acquisitions work and some don't?* Identify those reasons and not only will you be rich, you'll also make the entire economy more efficient."

"That's true," Derek said.

"So I've told you how to get rich and how to change the world," Mr. Bensen said. "Anything else you want to know before we bring out the cupcakes and 2-liters?"

"Actually, I was watching a show the other day—you've got me watching these financial news programs. *Derivatives*. Do you use them? They were trashing them on the show. Are they bad? What are they exactly?" Derek asked.

"They're like dynamite," Mr. Bensen said. "Use them right and they'll make your job easy. Misuse them and you might blow yourself up. We use them all the time. For example, we buy orange juice futures. If orange juice goes up in price we're in real trouble."

"Why's that?"

"Orange juice is one of the main ingredients in Caspian Sea," Mr. Bensen explained.

Derek's face flushed hot and he choked on a big gulp.

"You okay?" Mr. Bensen asked.

"Sorry," Derek said. "I've still got that guy Moss in my head—he was all about getting the ingredients to the drink."

"He told you it was a national security threat right?" Mr. Bensen asked. "Nuts. So, yeah, there's the mystery. Orange juice. Caspian Sea is purple, it does have plums in it, but it's about 80% orange juice. If there's a freeze in Florida and prices rise we could be in real trouble, so we enter futures contracts. We agree today to buy a certain amount of orange juice at some time in the future for a set price. That's called *going long*. We can lock prices in for the next three years or so.

"Meanwhile, there's an orange grower who is short orange juice futures. He's afraid that prices will go down. He can lock in the price at which he will sell. We can lock in the price at which we will buy. Both of us have eliminated some uncertainty to our business. Both of us can sleep better. That's one way financial markets make life better.

"There are other kinds of derivatives like options and swaps but we don't use them," Mr. Bensen said. "A derivative is any financial asset that *derives* its value from the value of another asset. Nothing too scary.

"Anything else?" Mr. Bensen asked.

"What's in the other 20%?" Derek asked and laughed. "No. Please. Don't tell me. I'd never sleep if I knew that."

"I don't even know what's in the other 20%," Mr. Bensen said. "Don't care." He finished off his milkshake.

Derek finished his off too. "Thanks again," he said.

"My pleasure," Mr. Bensen said and grinned.

"I really appreciate the time," Derek said, "and all the work. I've actually had fun—even without the whole espionage adventure. Lots of folks think Finance is boring but I think it's because they don't understand it. Not that I understand all of it, but it's been fun getting my head around this stuff."

"You do have a knack for it too—that helps. You know, we've barely scratched the surface. Now that you know the basics you can start on the really fun stuff—not just fun, but meaningful, and rewarding." Mr. Bensen said and stood and looked out the window. "Seriously. Maximizing shareholder wealth sounds cold and heartless to some, but not to me. I think about Alex and Spencer and the angel investors, even the venture capitalist guys. They believed in me. They trusted me with their capital, their retirement. Now there are all kinds of people who depend on the Caspian Sea money machine. I want the best for them. There's a reward, beyond money, in doing right by those people. They're people."

Derek looked at the back of Mr. Bensen's head when he finished talking. He wondered if there were tears in his eyes.

Mr. Bensen turned around—no tears. He picked up the envelope from the table and handed it to Derek. "Here. Here's a final list of things to think about. Some facts, some questions, some answers. Make sure you take a look at it all." He walked toward Derek and Derek stood up. They shook hands.

"Seriously, thank you," Derek said. "For everything."

10.1

Derek checked his phone for texts when he walked out of the building. "5:00 :)" He had time to kill. He crossed the street and walked, cautiously, over toward the hedge that the man with the sweat pants had been hiding behind. He tried to look through and peek around the hedge—he couldn't see anything. He wondered if anyone was watching from surrounding windows. He walked by the hedge—no one was there.

He's probably grabbing a sandwich somewhere—or a cup of coffee. I've gotta buy coffee again today. I'm gonna need some income if these cups of coffee become regular—if they turn into dinners and nights out. It feels different not having a $10,000 cushion. During the pizza discussion the week before, Derek thought it was important to tell the lawyer that he'd received one payment from Stovall. Mr. Bensen, the lawyer, and Molly were all impressed that Derek hadn't touched the money. Derek understood, but he was disappointed when the lawyer said, "You're gonna have to give that back—we'll help you handle it."

Derek checked his watch. 4:15 pm. He still had time to kill. The air was nice. He walked over to the park. He walked up to the empty bench, looked around, and sat. He leaned back, relaxed, and squinted up into the sun peeking through the breeze-blown leaves. He closed his eyes for a second and took several deep breaths. *Might as well check out my last set of homework.* He sat up and leaned forward a little and tore open the top of the manila envelope. *He didn't say ... I guess he wants me to drop this stuff by next week sometime.*

There was only a letter-sized Caspian Sea envelope, sealed, with Derek's name printed on it. He opened the envelope carefully and pulled out a two-page letter. When he unfolded the letter, a check dropped out. $1,000. The check was made out to Derek. On the memo line it said "Trouble."

Derek read the letter. It was a job offer. All terms were "to be determined" and were contingent upon Derek Foster's ability to graduate from college "with the following grade point average _____." Derek would have to write in that required GPA. He read everything over, shaking his head. As long as he graduated with the GPA he would set, he had a job at Caspian Sea. He was stunned. He pulled out his phone to call his mother. The phone buzzed. "Finished early. On my way down." He shoved everything back in the big envelope and stood and hurried out of the park toward the coffee shop. *I'll tell Molly first.*

A FINAL NOTE

This is not the end of Finance; it's the beginning. You know the basics. Next it will be time to do deeper, more realistic analysis of the three decisions in Finance. Reality is messy and answers are elusive but a deeper understanding will allow you to add value to a firm and to society and to your bank account. Below are some final comments on the three decisions.

Financing Decision—You can describe how stocks and bonds work and you can estimate their value. The question remains: should a firm raise money by issuing stock or bonds? Nobel prizewinners, Franco Modigliani and Merton Miller, demonstrated that it does not matter in a perfect world. Of course, they realized the world is not perfect. This irrelevance proposition is a starting point. Allowing firms to deduct interest payments from taxable income make debt more attractive. The possibility of bankruptcy makes debt less attractive. Information asymmetry, risk, and other factors may or may not make debt or equity more or less attractive. The goal of the firms is to maximize shareholder wealth. Minimizing the firm's WACC helps maximize shareholder wealth. What mix of debt and equity does that? There is no textbook with a definite answer, only informed judgments based on an understanding of core principles and market imperfections.

Investment Decision—You can find the NPV and IRR of any project. However, all the inputs to the decision process are based on estimates—estimates of the firm's WACC, futures sales, future costs, etc. Bad estimates lead to bad decisions. You know that if the NPV is positive, then accept the project; if it is negative the reject it. The rules you learned did not consider flexibility or strategic reasoning. The ability to abandon, expand, or delay a project was not considered. These are examples of real options. They add a layer of complexity to the investment decision. A negative NPV project might have some competitive or strategic benefit that was not considered in the cash flow analysis. The goal of the firm is to maximize shareholder wealth. All the effects of a project must be considered. There is no convenient check list.

Dividend Decision—Modigliani and Miller show that this decision does not matter either—in a perfect world. Investors who want cash can invest in a firm that pays dividends. If the firm doesn't pay dividends then they could sell some shares. Either way they get the money they need. Firms that need cash can keep earnings or issue new securities. Either way they get the money they need. Taxes affect the investor's decision. The cost of paying investment bankers to issue new securities affects the firm's decision. Dividends might be a signal that management feels confident in the firm's ability to make generate cash in the future. The goal of the firm is to maximize shareholder wealth. What dividend payment does that? There is no textbook with a definite answer, only informed judgments based on an understanding of core principles and market imperfections.

CPSIA information can be obtained at www.ICGtesting.com
Printed in the USA
LVOW10s2010211114

414961LV00002B/3/P